CW00820387

THE ⚡⚡ OF TREBLINKA

THE SS OF TREBLINKA

IAN BAXTER

SPELLMOUNT

First published in 2010
by Spellmount, an imprint of The History Press
The Mill, Brimscombe Port
Stroud, Gloucestershire, GL5 2QG
www.thehistorypress.co.uk

British Library Cataloguing in Publication Data.
A catalogue record for this book is available from the British Library.

ISBN 978 0 7524 4995 1

Typesetting and origination by The History Press
Printed in Great Britain

'If there is ever a generation after us which is so wet and weak-kneed that it does not understand our great task then the whole of National Socialism will have been in vain.'

SS-Oberstgruppenführer Odilo Globocnik, summer of 1942.

Dedicated to my dear nephew Albie and niece Lilly – hoping they ensure that future generations never repeat such inhumanity again.

Contents

Glossary and Abbreviations

Einsatzgruppen	Mobile killing units of the SS, Sipo–SD
Gau	One of the 42 Nazi Party administrative districts into which Nazi Germany was divided
Gauleiter	Nazi Party boss in a *gau*
Gestapo	*Geheime Staatspolizei*: state secret police
Kapo	Privileged prisoner who served as a barracks supervisor/warder or leader of a work detail in a Nazi concentration camp, labour camp or death camp
Reichsführer-SS	Reich Chief of the SS and German Police
RSHA	*Reichssicherheitshauptamt*: Reich Main Security Office, formed in late 1939, uniting Gestapo, criminal police, SIPO and SD
SD	*Sicherheitsdienst*: security service of the Nazi Party
Sonderkommando	Special unit of SS
SS	*Schutzstaffel*: Guard Detachment created in 1925 as elite Nazi Party bodyguard that evolved into a security and intelligence service with a military arm
Totenkopf	*Totenkopfverbande*: Death's Head, unit of SS deployed to guard concentration camps
Waffen-SS	Weapon SS: Military arm of the SS from 1939 onwards
Wehrmacht	German armed forces
WVHA	*Wirtschaffts und Verwaltungshauptamt*: SS Economic and Administrative Head Office, responsible for SS economic enterprises and concentration camps from 1942 under the command of Oswald Pohl

Preface

By the time Treblinka was made fully operational in July 1942, the SS had built a killing factory capable of exterminating hundreds of thousands of people, which could be run by a handful of men.

This book explains and charts the decisions that led to the sophistication of a killing system that delivered families to their deaths by a railway link that stopped only metres from the gas chambers. It shows the individual SS-men during their murderous activities inside the camp, and reveals them relaxing in their barracks or visiting the camp zoo. With the aid of photographs and personal letters it provides a chilling portrayal of the creators and administrators of Treblinka.

Treblinka is perhaps one of the least famous concentration camps, and yet during its short operation some 800,000 Jews were murdered at the camp. Informed by recently discoverd material, some of which has never been published before, this book exposes the inner workings of the camp – from the technical 'challenges' of mass murder to the everyday lives of the killers.

The Author

Ian Baxter is a military historian who specialises in German twentieth century military history. He has written more than twenty books including: *Wolf's Lair: Inside Hitler's East Prussian HQ*, *The Eighteen Day Victory March*, *Panzers In North Africa*, *The Ardennes Offensive*, *The Western Campaign*, *The 12th SS Panzer-Division Hitlerjugend*, *The Waffen-SS on the Western Front*, *The Waffen-SS on the Eastern Front*, *The Red Army at Stalingrad*, *Elite German Forces of World War II*, *Armoured Warfare*, *German Tanks of War*, *Blitzkrieg*, *Panzer-Divisions At War*, *Hitler's Panzers*, *German Armoured Vehicles of World War Two*, *Last Two Years of the Waffen-SS At War*, *German Soldier Uniforms and Insignia*, *German Guns of the Third Reich*, *Defeat to Retreat: The Last Years of the German Army At War 1943–1945*, *Operation Bagration – the Destruction of Army Group Centre*, *Rommel and the Afrika Korps*, *The Sixth Army and the Road to Stalingrad*, *Battle of the Baltics 1944–1945*, *The last years of the Panzerwaffe 1943–1945*, *The Hitlerjugend 1934–1945*, *Women Concentration Camp Guards*, and *Rudolf Höss, the Creator of Auschwitz*. He has written over one hundred journal articles including: 'Last days of Hitler', 'Story of the V1 and V2 rocket programme', 'Secret Aircraft of World War Two', 'Rommel at Tobruk', 'Secret British Plans To Assassinate Hitler', 'SS At Arnhem', 'Battle Of Caen 1944', 'Gebirgsjäger At War', 'Panzer Crews', '*Hitlerjugend* Guerrillas', 'Last Battles in the East', and 'Battle of Berlin'. He has also reviewed numerous military studies for publication, supplied thousands of photographs and important documents to various publishers and film production companies worldwide. He lectures to schools, colleges and universities throughout the United Kingdom and Ireland. He lives in Essex, England.

Introduction

The suffering that Nazi Germany inflicted on the Jews has been well documented. However, material relating to the daily lives of the SS men in the death camps is almost non-existent. After the war, most were of course anxious to cover up their past and were hardly likely to sit down in a prison cell and start recording their memoirs. Even at their trials, when many of the perpetrators were forced to confess to their dreadful actions, very little was revealed about their thoughts and experiences. One exception in this regard was Franz Stangl, the second commandant of the Treblinka death camp. As commandant, Stangl was imprisoned for life. Gitta Sereny, who had covered his trial on behalf of a London newspaper, became fascinated by the prisoner and decided to conduct a series of interviews with him in order to know him better, and to delve into his mind. She also interviewed his wife, his children, his friends, his accomplices, and victims in order to build a portrait of this death camp coordinator.

It was through reading Gitta Sereny's book, *Into that Darkness; From Mercy Killing to Mass Murder, A Study of Franz Stangl, the Commandant of Treblinka* that I first became fascinated by the SS of Treblinka. The book was an appalling insight into the mind of the commandant, and for me its power came from its historical description of a man that was no mere robot blindly following orders, but a character eager to adapt and improvise and efficiently carry out the task he was given. Like many SS-men he found that eventually, as the systematic slaughter of the Jews increased, all consciousness of individual guilt diminished, and murder was simply an administrative procedure. Yet, throughout all these killings many of the key figures remained mysterious figures to me. As a result I decided, after much deliberation, to immerse myself in researching the Treblinka death camp, concentrating not so much on the victims, but those responsible for their murder.

Through books and documentary material I dug deep to unravel the complexities of the organization, construction and evolution of Treblinka, the largest of the five Nazi exterminations camps. I was determined from the onset to find out what made the perpetrators do what they did; even the first commandant, *SS-Obersturmführer* Dr Irmfried Eberl, was secretly competing with other camps to achieve the highest number of exterminations.

I wanted to know what life was like for the SS working inside the camp; to try and understand their feelings and experiences and behaviour, not only towards their victims, but their family and loved ones as well. I found to my surprise that the personnel who ran Treblinka and supervised the exterminations were apparently 'ordinary' people. They were not assigned their tasks because of any type of exceptional qualities they had. Their anti-Semitism was part of their culture that had been nurtured over years of intense propaganda. Most were married, and the majority did not have a criminal record. They had simply volunteered to serve in the SS in a death camp where they were ordered to carry out their duties loyally and unquestioningly. They had *chosen* to exhibit terrible cruelty toward their victims. When these men were not physically and mentally abusing the prisoners they were exterminating thousands each day.

Unlike Auschwitz, Treblinka did not evolve into an extermination camp. It was built for one purpose, to murder. The death camp needed relatively few facilities of any kind, and could be contained in a small space. Visitors to Treblinka, and there were not many, were shocked by how tiny the killing camp was. The SS had embarked on something that human beings had never attempted before – the mechanized extermination of thousands of men, women and children. Treblinka gives us a chance to examine how human beings behaved in a situation that pushed human transgression to its furthest reaches. From this history there is a great deal we can learn about ourselves. It is very easy to think of the SS at Treblinka as monsters. But to actually see them leading a relatively normal existence is somehow more disturbing because it relates them to us. The murders at Treblinka raise some profound questions regarding the human capacity for evil. Throughout my research I found that the perpetrators as a whole were not sadists lusting for power and blood, or brainwashed by propaganda, or simply following orders. They had exercised a personal choice to be or not to be, evil. Many chose to be ruthless and brutal, like Eberl, who actually promoted the use of violence and terror 'beyond the call of duty'.

Through examining many diaries and various documents, I discovered that the SS posted to Treblinka wrote about their personal experiences as if they were 'normal'. Nowhere do they present themselves as mindless automatons that just followed orders. Although they were massively influenced by the propaganda of the times, it is quite evident that they nevertheless made a series of personal choices. They carried on working at Treblinka not just because they were ordered to, but because being posted to a concentration camp meant they would avoid any risk to life, most importantly, they would not be fighting on a battlefield in southern Russia. There is no definite record of any member of the SS refusing to work in the camp. They could have easily rejected the posting and been sent to the front, but they were content living in the camp and killing those they regarded as having no intrinsic claim to life.

Many of the SS men regarded their posting to Treblinka as a boon, and certainly felt what they were doing there was right. Although they were taught blind and absolute obedience to all orders from their SS superiors, there were a number of occasions when some felt emboldened to criticize the way the camp was being run. Like other SS men in the concentration camp system they seldom needed to fear reprisal if they criticized an order because their superiors often allowed officers lower down the chain of command openly to use their initiative and voice their views. Commanders knew that many of the SS men believed wholeheartedly in the overall Nazi vision, and for this reason they were relatively free to question the details of how the camp was run.

According to documents and various correspondences along the SS chains of command, some personnel openly voiced their views about the conditions and overcrowding. They were not concerned about the killing of the Jews, but worried about the efficiency of the killing machine itself. There were numerous complaints filed from the SS outlining the immense workload, and there were deep concerns about potential disorder and a breakdown in morale among the guards. Eberl received a litany of complaints from his subordinates. But they found that Eberl, like severall other concentration camp commandants, looked upon his SS colleagues with suspicion, hostility, even hatred. His ambition was not the welfare of his staff or the smooth running of the factory, but to reach the highest possible numbers of gassed victims and exceed the 'output' of the other camps.

Yet off duty his subordinates saw a completely different side to Eberl. He would regularly invite his staff for drinks where they would be accommodated most cordially. He was a most hospitable host and everyone was mightily impressed with his conduct. Many of the SS-men at Treblinka had manufactured for themselves what they considered to be a tolerable life. Outside the camp they felt more or less insulated from the brutality, and when they walked through the forest crossing the main railway line that led directly to the camp, they were able to avert from their eyes anything that displeased them. Almost every SS man was determined from the outset to conceal as much of the gruesome knowledge they all had as possible. In their mind's eye it was not just their oath they were protecting, but their own credentials as human beings.

Many of the SS whilst serving in the camp were inspired by the thought of home, believing that when they got leave they would be able recapture the life they had possessed before their posting. But it was not possible. Treblinka had altered them. Though they never sought to change their comfortable existence in the camp, the psychological burden they had to carry manifested itself. They deliberately manipulated and repressed their moral scruples. Many of them had an intense desire to tell the truth, especially to those close to them. But the majority felt bound by honour and duty to the SS order, and were compelled to carry out their crimes in secret. The psychological impact on some of them was often severe, despite being exposed on a daily basis to the horrors. Some SS men actually did try to avoid working.

From sifting through personal diaries and testimonies that were exposed during the trials, it seems that most of the SS, particularly young new recruits, felt it essential to comfort themselves with the idea that they had no choice but to do their duty, in whatever evil capacity. But at the same time they found it necessary to create in themselves a capacity for dissociation to some extent from the horrors of Treblinka. It was ruthlessness that normally enabled an individual to accept what he was doing was right. Although most openly agreed with the process of murder at the camp, they were aware of the grave consequences if they were to lose the war. They were not so much concerned with their own moral scruples, but more disturbed by the implications if caught by the enemy.

In the last months at Treblinka in 1943, known as 'phase four' of the camp, the SS had begun to realize what it would mean if the war was lost and the outside world learned of what had been done in Treblinka. It was during this time that a number of SS men forced themselves to be slightly more affable with the prisoners. They tried to make make use of individual prisoners hoping one day they would speak in their defence. Those few SS that were more helpful beyond this aim had a conscience, despite trying to bury their innermost feelings. Even commandant Stangl himself felt a kind of pity for the Jews, but could never look them full in the face. He attempted to repress it all by creating a fantasy simulacrum of normality, planting gardens, building barracks, kitchens, barbers, tailors, and shoemakers. But in the end, for him, as he admtted himself, the only way to deal with it was to drink. He took a large brandy to bed with him each night.

Although he rarely saw the Jews as individuals, he scrupulously avoided talking to those who were about to die. As soon as the condemned were in the undressing barracks, and as soon as they were naked, they were no longer human beings for him. What he was avoiding, like many of his subordinates, was witnessing the transition. When he cited instances of interaction with prisoners, it was never with any of those who were about to die.

At home, Stangl bore secrets. He told his wife that he was the highest ranking officer in Treblinka, but failed to reveal to her he was actually Commandant. His job, he said, was only administrative, 'but at least I was not at the front'. Frau Stangl knew that Treblinka was a concentration camp, but according to her she never knew there were children, or even women there. Like so many other Germans she tried to rationalize it and told herself that they were killing men who were the enemies of the State. She even convinced herself that the women and children were being left at home. She refused to believe any of it, because that would have made her husband a cold-blooded murderer.

Treblinka as we know became the largest extermination centre, outstripping Auschwitz. But as the reader will learn the actual process of extermination at Treblinka was far from ideal, and this caused the SS many problems, not just from an administrative perspective, but an 'engineering' one. As in any industrial operation, all the machinery had to be working together for the required end result. When Rudolf Höss, Commandant of Auschwitz, arrived at the camp in July 1942 to see for himself the running of the camp and the extermination facility, it was clear to him that the camp was struggling with the high frequency of transports. In Höss's opinion, Treblinka was not a very efficient camp. The gas chambers at Auschwitz, though only recently installed at this time, were much larger, and unlike the commandant of Treblinka, Höss did not waste valuable time and resources killing Jews with exhaust gas. Also, the victims arriving at Treblinka were aware of their impending deaths, whereas at Auschwitz the victims were duped into believing that they were simply going through a delousing process. The chaos caused by the backlog of trains waiting to take the victims through to be killed and the panic and disorder that followed when they were unloaded off the cattle trucks caused not only a collapse in the smooth running of the operation, but a breakdown in the morale of the SS as well. As a result the SS began indiscriminately killing panicking mothers and their offspring in front of other frightened and bewildered Jews. Those queuing to go through into the gas chambers were also shot simply in order to try and reduce the backlog.

Astonishingly, Eberl was actually breaking Nazi law in not handling the mass killings more efficiently. Competent commandants, like Höss, would never have tolerated Jews being shot out of hand because officials were simply incapable of managing the gassing facility more effectively.

Chapter I

Plans for Genocide

Long before the defeat of Poland, Adolf Hitler had planned the large-scale annexation of the doomed country. When victory swiftly came at the end of September 1939, the Germans acquired territory with a population of over 20 million, of whom 17 million were Poles and 675,000 Germans. Hitler had decided to incorporate large areas of Poland into the Reich and clear the Poles and Jews out of the incorporated areas replacing them with German settlers. What followed was a period of more or less unrestrained terror in Poland in the incorporated territories. The areas that were not incorporated had a population of some 11 million. They comprised the Polish province of Lublin and parts of the provinces of Warsaw and Krakow. It was initially termed the 'General Government of the Occupied Polish Areas', but in 1940 was renamed the 'General Government'. This large unincorporated area was deemed the dumping ground for all undesirables and those considered enemies of the State. It was here that the first deportations of Poles and Jews were sent in their thousands.

During the first cold months of 1940 the General Government absorbed thousands of homeless and penniless people in an area that was already over-populated. In their place came thousands of ethnic Germans moving into the newly incorporated territories, all of which had to be provided with suitable housing. The scale of the relocation was enormous and chaotic.

By February the immense problems of simultaneously attempting to relocate Poles, Jews and the ethnic Germans had become such an administrative nightmare that it was agreed that the Jews should be forced to live in ghettos. This would not only relieve the burden of the resettlement programme, but it was a way of temporarily getting rid of the growing Jewish problem. Isolating them in ghettos was deemed immediately practicable not least because it was believed that Eastern Jews in particular were carriers of diseases, and needed to be isolated for that reason alone.

Whilst plans were put into practice to create the ghettos, the SS pursued harsh policies in order to deal with the threat of subversion by Polish nationalists and Jewish 'Bolshevists' in the newly incorporated territories. Already by early 1940 the situation in the various detention centres and concentration camps had become untenable due to the new policies of arresting and detaining enemies of the State. News had already circulated through SS channels that government officials were demanding immediate expansion of the concentration camp system through its newly conquered territory, Poland. The German authorities quickly pressed forward to establish various camps in Poland where Jews and other enemies of the State could be incarcerated and set to work as stonebreakers and construction workers. It was envisaged that these Poles would remain as a slave labour force, and it was therefore deemed necessary to erect these so called 'quarantine camps'.

Initially, it had been proposed that the 'quarantine camps' were to hold the prisoners until they were sent to the various other concentration camps in the Reich. However, it soon became apparent that this was totally impracticable so it was decided that these camps would function as a permanent prison for all those that were sent there.

Throughout 1940 the SS concentration camp system in Poland began to expand. In April a new camp was erected in the town of Oswiecim, which was situated in a remote corner of south-western Poland, in a marshy valley where the Sola River flows into the Vistula about 35 miles west of the ancient city of Krakow. The town was virtually unknown outside Poland and following the occupation of the country Oswiecim was incorporated into the Reich together with Upper Silesia and renamed by the German authorities Auschwitz.

Auschwitz was technically deemed a quarantine camp for labour exchange. The nearby town and surrounding area was to be expanded beyond all recognition. *SS-Reichsführer* Heinrich Himmler envisaged that a German settlement at Auschwitz would be built, and from this model town a Germanization of various villages would be effected.

When the Germans unleashed their attack against the Soviet Union on 22 June 1941, the Jewish problem escalated. For the Nazi empire the prospect of a war against Russia entailed a transition from one policy of murder to another, far more ambitious. It engendered the most radical ideas imaginable in the minds of the SS. As Hitler had explained to his generals just a few months prior to the invasion, the war would be no normal war; it was an 'ideological war' of extermination. In the eyes of Hitler the Soviet Union represented the home of Bolshevism and international Jewry, which needed to be rooted out and destroyed.

> Knowledge of the Jews is the only key whereby one may understand the inner nature and therefore the real aims of Social Democracy. The man who has come to know this race has succeeded in removing from his eyes the veil through which he had seen the aims and meaning of his Party in a false light; and then, out of the murk and fog of social phrases rises the grimacing figure of Marxism ... The Jewish doctrine of Marxism repudiates the aristocratic principle of Nature and substitutes for it the eternal privilege of force and energy, numerical mass and its dead weight. Thus it denies the individual worth of the human personality, impugns the teaching that nationhood and race have a primary significance, and by doing this it takes away the very foundations of human existence and human civilization. If the Marxist teaching were to be accepted as the foundation of the life of the universe, it would lead to the disappearance of all order that is conceivable to the human mind. And thus the adoption of such a law would provoke chaos in the structure of the greatest organism that we know, with the result that the inhabitants of this earthly planet would finally disappear. Should the Jew, with the aid of his Marxist creed, triumph over the people of this world, his Crown will be the funeral wreath of mankind, and this planet will once again follow its orbit through ether, without any human life on its surface, as it did millions of years ago. (Hitler, *Mein Kampf*)

This was a matter of life and death; the very survival of the human race depended on an answer to 'the Jewish question'.

To deal with the Jews in Russia four *Einsatzgruppen* (Action Groups) were formed that consisted of *Sipo-SD* personnel, *Waffen-SS* units, and police. Progress through the Soviet heartlands was swift and a massacre of the Jewish population ensued. Although the killing of the Jews by shooting proved effective in terms of the large numbers murdered, commanders in the field soon became aware it had many disadvantages as a method of mass murder. Firstly, the killings were difficult to conceal and were often witnessed by large numbers of unauthorized persons including the *Wehrmacht*, which sometimes complained about the brutality. This was not so much out of sympathy for those being executed but because of the psychological effects it had on the men. The stress it caused among many of the participants was such that it often led to soldiers consuming large amounts of alcohol whilst they killed. Others had nervous breakdowns, and there were numerous suicides. Some men simply could not face the strain and refused to take part in the slaughter. These men were regarded as weak and were quickly weeded out by their commanding officers and posted elsewhere to the front. They might have been deemed by their superiors as cowards, but no one was directly punished for such refusal – apart from the consequence of being sent to the thick of the fighting. For every soldier that refused to take part in the killings, there was always another to replace him. Virtually all men accepted their orders automatically, and soon became accustomed to the daily butchery of men, women and children.

At higher levels, there were occasional objections; especially from the *Wehrmacht*, but these complaints were generally politically or tactically motivated. Himmler made it clear to the *Wehrmacht* that they would have to simply accept the wholesale liquidations in the East as policy. It was a matter of ideology supervening over military or economic needs and for this reason they would have to accept it and cooperate. On 1 August, when his Brigade received the 'explicit order' from *Reichsführer-SS* (Himmler): 'All male Jews must be shot – drive the female Jews into the swamps', the then *Sturmbannführer der Reserve*, Commander of the mounted branch of 1.SS Cavalry Regiment Gustave Lombard was quick to disseminate the policy. 'No male Jew survives; no leftover familes remain the in the villages.'

Whilst the *Wehrmacht* accepted the killings in the East, the SS were aware that they needed a better technique to murder large numbers as quickly and as anonymously as possible. One idea, which was utilized in 1941, was to give the nastiest and most degrading jobs to the 'inferior' races, 'in order to preserve the psychic balance of our people', the Poles, Ukrainians, Balts and Jews, who were already destined to be killed. This was found to be an effectve policy, especially when rounding up and killing women and children.

However, it did not solve the problem of murdering ever greater numbers of people. They needed something cheaper, tidier and quicker, which would also be less distressing to the executioners. Even the *Reichsführer* was all too well aware of the problems of mass execution. In fact, in August 1941, whilst near Minsk he witnessed a mass killing and nearly fainted during the spectacle. He commented to a commander in the field that the execution was not humane and would lower the morale of the troops. He made it clear he wanted a more effective method of killing, such as explosives or gas.

The use of gas was not a new method at this time. A special department known as T4, which had organized the 'Euthanasia Programme', first used gassing installations in Germany to kill the insane and metnally handicapped. The programme was considered a complete success and ran for two years, but owing to growing public objections to euthanasia in Germany the killings were suspended, reluctantly. Now, it was proposed that this method of killing should be used outside Germany against enemies of the State, especially those from the East. The invasion of the Soviet Union in the summer of 1941 gave access to thousands of Jews and other groups regarded by the Nazis as 'subhuman', and plans were quickly enacted to use gas.

Over the coming weeks whilst the *Wehrmacht* continued to advance ever deeper into Russia, gas was introduced for the first time to the *Einsatzgruppen*. A special vehicle had been built to resemble an ambulance or refrigerator truck that was air tight. The victims would be placed in the cabin and carbon monoxide was introduced by means of a pipe. By the autumn of 1941, the first gas van prepared for the Eastern Front was tested on Russian prisoners of war in Sachsenhausen concentration camp. This crude method of systematic annihilation of human beings was considered the best and most effective means of mass killing whilst the troops pushed forward through the Soviet Union. It was also deemed to help the special commando killing squads because they never need look into the eyes of their victims as they had when they gunned them down.

Dr Albert Wildmann of the RSHA's Criminal Technical Institute described how the new method was decided upon.

After only a brief period, the commandos of the *Einsatzgruppen* got into considerable difficulties. The members of the *Einsatz* – and special commandos, some of whom were themselves fathers, were in the long run not up to the mental strain caused by the mass shootings, particularly when women and children were involved. There were disputes, refusals to obey orders, drunken orgies, but also serious psychological illness. Himmler, who was at first not aware of the situation was looking for a way of reducing the nervous psychological strain on the men involved in the shooting. Thus, in discussions with Heydrich and other leading figures the plan emerged of utilizing gas vans for this purpose, which were to be used for the liquidation of women and children in particular ... In September or October 1941, the head of Department IID in the RSHA, *SS Obersturmbannführer* Rauff, was ordered by Heydrich to build gas vans.[1]

Although many thousands of Jews and Russians were captured and herded into the new gas vans and murdered, the vans were not very popular with the SS since they were deemed unpleasant to operate, worse than mass executions by shooting. However, they were to remain the preferred method of liquidating the Jews in Russia.

Gas vans were also used in the first extermination centre which was built in the nearby village of Chelmno. The first transport of Jews arrived in lorries on 5 December 1941. Over a five month period some 55,000 Jews from the nearby Lodz ghetto were gassed along with at least 5,000 Gypsies.

Whist the Chelmno extermination centre had been geared to the liquidation of the Jews in the surrounding district in the Warthegau, the vast majority of Polish Jews, including many deported or who had fled from the Warthegau, were in the General Government area. A total of some 2,300,000 were now contained in ghettos there.

At the Wannsee conference held in Berlin in January 1942, it was agreed that it would be the Jews in the General Government that would be dealt with first. In fact, preparations had already been undertaken and the Nazi leadership was under no illusion that it required great organizational skills to commit mass murder. Already a pool of experts had been drafted in to undertake this mammoth task. The Wannsee Conference, presided over by *Generalleutnant* Reinhard Heydrich involved fourteen representatives of the military and governmental departments that would be most closely concerned with the Final Solution to the Jewish question. Attending were *Gauleiter* Dr Alfred Meyer and *Reichamtsleiter* (Chief Officer); Dr Georg Leibrandt – Reich Ministry for the Occupied Eastern Territories; State Secretary Dr Wilhelm Stuckart – Reich Ministry of the Interior;

State Secretary Dr Erich Neumann – Office of the Plenipotentiary of the Four Year Plan; State Secretary Dr Roland Freisler – Reich Justice Ministry; State Secretary Dr Josef Bühler – Office of Governor General (Poland) representing Hans Frank; *SS-Oberführer* Gerhard Klopfer – Party Chancellery representing Martin Bormann; Ministerial Director Friedrich Kritzinger – Reich Chancellery; SS Major-General Otto Hofmann – Race and Resettlement Main Office; SS Major-General Heinrich Müller – Reich Security Main Office; SS Lt-Colonel Adolf Eichmann – Reich Security Main Office; Under State Secretary Martin Luther – Foreign Office; SS Senior-Colonel Dr Eberhard Schöngarth – Commander of the Security Police and the SD in the General Government (Poland); and SS Major Dr Rudolf Lange – Commander of Security Police and Security Service for General Commissariat Latvia, as Deputy of Commanding Officer of Security Police and Security Service for Reich Commissariat *Ostland* (the Baltic States and White Russia) Security Police and Security Service.

We know from the minutes of the meeting that there was no ambiguity about that 'Solution'. Having listed the number of Jews living in each country, Heydrich stated in the minutes, or protocol:

In large, single-sex labour columns, Jews fit to work will work their way eastwards constructing roads. Doubtless the large majority will be eliminated by natural causes. Any final remnant that survives will doubtless consist of the most resistant elements. They will have to be dealt with appropriately because otherwise, by natural selection, they would form the germ cell of a new Jewish revival.

They would have to be eliminated.

From the onset they were aware that transporting large numbers of Jews to Russia and liquidating them there would be a logistical nightmare, especially when the war in Russia had not been won. They soon came to the conclusion that it was more practical to transport German and other Jews to Poland and to kill them immediately, rather than send them farther East. It was therefore suggested that a series of extermination camps would be constructed in Poland and used primarily to take those who were deemed unfit for work to be killed.

The preparation for the extermination of the Jews in Poland had been rubberstamped at the Wannsee Conference. In Berlin a special organization, later named 'Operation Reinhard', was established. Operation Reinhard was the code name given for the systematic annihilation of the Polish Jews in the General Government territories, and it would mark the beginning of the use of extermination camps. The SS and Police Leader of the district of Lublin, *SS-Oberstgruppenführer* Odilo Globocnik, was appointed the commander of the operation. Globocnik was a ruthless and fanatical SS officer who believed wholeheartedly in the Nazi vision. From his office he planned and gossiped with his associates about the future SS colonization of the East and the task of preparing for the extermination of the Jews in the General Government.

Globocnik set to work immediately and brought in people that had been assigned to the euthanasia programme that had knowledge of and experience in setting up and operating systems for mass murder. The construction of three death camps was planned, with sites at Belzec, Sobibor and Treblinka.

The first of the Operation Reinhard extermination camps in Poland was located in the south-east of the district of Lublin called Belzec. The camp was situated 500 metres from the station siding. It was divided into two parts; Camp I on the north-west side containing the reception area with two barracks – one for undressing and where the women had their hair shorn and the other one for storing clothes and luggage. Camp II comprised the gas chambers, a large area for the mass graves, and two barracks for the Jewish work details, one as living quarters and one containing a kitchen. The gas chambers were surrounded by trees and had camouflage nets on the roof. Camps I and II were divided by a wire fence. The barrack for undressing and the gas chambers were linked by a path two metres wide and 57 metres long, known as the 'tube', which was concealed on each side by a wire fence and foliage. The whole camp was topped with barbed wire and camouflaged with newly planted conifers. On each side the camp was overlooked by two wooden watch towers.

The entire camp was to be guarded by around 80 guards, all of whom were Ukrainian. Famed for their brutality, many were trained by the Germans and allowed this opportunity to escape the terrible conditions of the POW camps. They were all trained at Travniki, a special camp near Lublin specifically set up to prepare and train Ukrainians and ethnic Germans for their role in *Aktion Reinhard*. These volunteers were nicknamed by the local population 'Trawniki men' or 'Askaris'. The Germans called them *Hilfswillige* ('volunteer helpers'), or 'Hiwis' for short (though the term was much more widely applicable, beyond the Trawniki men, to all locally recruited, non-German volunteers).

Some of the Ukrainian guards were organized into two battalions with four companies each, about 1,000 men altogether. The size of the company was roughly 100–200 men. One or two of the companies were stationed mainly in Lublin for security duties, whilst the others were sent mainly to guard labour camps in the Lublin district. Their duties comprised of supporting the local police units, carrying out deportations and mass executions of Jews. Their first assignment to the Reinhard camps was at Belzec where a company-size unit of around 100 men was sent.

The camp Commandant, Christian Wirth, had arrived at Belzec before Christmas 1941, bringing with him a group of about ten 'euthanasia' specialists, including the notorious chemist, Dr Kallmeyer. They had been given the task of constructing the gassing facility and then operating it. Killing people with gas was not new to Wirth. In 1939 he became involved in the euthanasia actions against the mentally ill or handicapped and assisted in the wholesale extermination of the victims using bottled carbon monoxide. Two years later, in 1941, he was dispatched to Lublin where he continued his killings. Wirth soon earned himself a reputation and was nicknamed 'savage Christian'. At Belzec Wirth ruled the camp with an iron fist and encouraged his SS personnel to commit terrible acts of brutality against their victims.

Within months of his arrival Wirth was adapting previous killing techniques with the use of gas. By February 1942 two gassing tests were undertaken at Belzec, the first with Zyklon B (hydrogen cyanide gas) and the second with bottled carbon monoxide. Among the victims of the second test were German-Jewish psychiatric patients deported from Germany and local Jews from Piaski and Izbica. As a cheaper alternative a Soviet tank engine was then installed outside the chambers to produce carbon monoxide from exhaust gas which was fed into the chamber. The experiment was a complete success and there was now no need for a constant supply of CO gas to a far distant part of Poland.

Wirth realized that by killing large numbers of people in one physical place he had broke completely from the conventional design of a concentration camp. Because the vast majority of arrivals would be alive only for a matter of a few hours, a large complex of wooden and concrete buildings, such as those found at Auschwitz, would not be required. A death camp, unlike a concentration camp, needed only a few facilities to operate effectively. It would require only a small space.

Wirth was aware that the smooth functioning of a death camp required more guile than a concentration camp. Whereas most prisoners that were sent to places like Auschwitz and Dachau knew that they were being incarcerated, at a death camp Wirth wanted to conceal the true purpose of the place from the new arrivals for as long as possible. So within the camp he had the gas chamber building camouflaged and hidden behind trees and a wire fence.

He knew that by building a large gas chamber the killing process would not only spare his own men from psychological 'suffering', but also more importantly it would mean fewer personnel would be required to actually run the camp. He would employ a number of healthy Jewish slave labourers that would be selected upon arrival to the camp and put to work burying bodies, sorting the vast quantities of clothing and valuables, and cleaning the gas chambers.

The Belzec death camp finally began its operations on 17 March 1942 with a transport of some 50 goods wagons containing Jews from Lublin. Between March and the end of April, thousands of Jews from the Lublin and Lemberg districts were successfully exterminated in Belzec. Himmler sent his congratulations to Wirth who had finally built a killing factory capable of murdering many hundreds of thousands of people in one single space. Wirth looked upon the operation as a director of a plant where the raw goods were delivered, processed and then stored. Wirth had realized his *Reichsführer's* dream that the desired result would finally be the complete annihilation of the Jewish race. Yet, the shrewd and evil Wirth knew that Belzec alone would not be sufficient to deal with the numbers of people scheduled to be sent there.

So, in March whilst the first trainloads of Jews were being readied for Belzec, another 'Reinhard' death camp was being constructed. It was near the small village of Sobibor in a wooded area on the Chelmno-Wlodawa railway line a few miles south of Wlodawa. The installation was an enlarged and improved version of Belzec with the same general layout. *SS-Hauptsturmführer* Franz Stangl, a 34-year-old Austrian graduate of Hartheim 'euthanasia' centre was appointed commandant. Stangl had been the son of a night-watchman and during the 1930s was accepted into the Austrian police service. Later, he claimed he liked the security and cleanliness that the Austrian police uniforms appeared to offer. After the *Anschluss*, Stangl was quickly promoted through the ranks. By 1940, through a direct order from Himmler, Stangl became superintendent of the T-4 Euthanasia Programme at the Euthanasia Institute at Schloss Hartheim. It was here at the centre that Stangl first met Wirth. According to Stangl,

> Wirth was a gross and florid man. My heart sank when I met him ... Whenever he was there, he addressed us daily at lunch. And here it was again, this awful verbal crudity: when he spoke about the necessity for this euthanasia operation, he wasn't speaking in humane or scientific terms, the way Dr Werner had described it to me.[2]

By the time Stangl received his new appointment Wirth had become commander of both Chelmno and Belzec, and was soon to oversee Stangl's operation at Sobibor.

Just prior to Stangl's appointment to Sobibor he had to report to the *SS* HQ in Lublin where he met *SS-Gruppenführer* Odilo Globocnik, who was directing the extermination of the Jews in Poland. For almost three hours on a park bench Globocnik went through the plans for the new camp, but never told Stangl that the new installation was an extermination centre for Jews. The order for building the camp was published on 16 December 1941, in the *Amtsblatt für den Distrikt Warschau Generalgouvernement*. (Official Gazette for the Warsaw district of the General Government.)

When Stangl arrived at Sobibor it still resembled a building site. Whilst he busied himself overseeing construction of the camp, he was informed that Wirth had been appointed inspector of the camps and that he had to report to him immediately. He journeyed by car to Belzec, which was now in full operation.

> As one arrived, one first reached Belsec railway station, on the left side of the road. The camp was on the same side, but up a hill. The *Kommandantur* was 200 metres away, on the other side of the road. It was a one storey building. The smell ... Oh my God, the smell. It was everywhere. Wirth wasn't in his office. I remember they took me to him ... he was standing on a hill, next to the pits ... the pits ... full ... they were full. I can't

tell you; not hundreds, thousands, thousands of corpses ... oh God. That's where Wirth told me – he said that was what Sobibor was for. And he was putting me officially in charge.[3]

When Wirth visited Belzec the camp was in already in turmoil. One of the pits was already overflowing with corpses and the putrefaction had progressed too fast, so that the liquid underneath had pushed the bodies to the surface of the earth and rolled down the hill. The gassing installation was perpetually breaking down and the deportees that were waiting to be gassed were left naked, without food or water, sometimes for days. Others were left crammed in the railway wagons, with many of them suffocating as a result, just a few hundred metres from the camp.

Wirth told Stangl that the problems at Belzec were caused by a massive influx of deportees, that the gas vans could simply not cope with such a huge number of people. Stangl was shocked at the terrible conditions and the suffering of those awaiting their fate outside the gas chambers. However, no matter how repugnant this was to him, he was armoured by the structure of allegiance and returned to Sobibor to undertake his duty as commandant of an extermination centre. A few days later Wirth arrived at the camp to oversee the completion of the gas chamber. Once the gas chamber had been completed Stangl was ordered to witness his first gassing.

When I got there, Wirth was standing in front of the building wiping the sweat off his cap and fuming. Michel told me later that he'd suddenly appeared, looked around the gas chambers on which they were still working and said, 'Right, we'll try it out now with those 25 work Jews: get them up here.' They marched our 25 Jews up there and just pushed them in and gassed them. Michel said Wirth behaved like a lunatic, hit out at his own staff with his whip to drive them on. And then he was livid because the doors hadn't worked properly.[4]

Yet, in front of his subordinates he appeared mightily impressed with the effectiveness of the gas chambers.

Stangl was shocked by the first gassing and was determined that he would try to avoid the graphic spectacle in future. In fact, when Sobibor officially became operational in mid-May 1942, he did just that. At Sobibor, he said,

… one could avoid seeing almost all of it – it all happened so far away from the camp-buildings. All I could think of was that I wanted to get out. I schemed and planned and planned. I heard there was a new police unit at Mogilec. I went again to Lublin and filled out an application form for transfer. I asked Hofle [*Hans Hofle, Deputy Director of Action Reinhard*] to help me get Globocnik's agreement. Two months later – in June – my wife wrote that she had been requested to supply details about the children's ages: they were going to be granted a visit to Poland.⁵

Despite Stangl's apparent inner misgivings about the camp operations they nonetheless accelerated at a tremendous rate. Within the first two months some 100,000 people were killed there. Often Stangl appeared at the unloading ramps dressed in white riding clothes watching as the Ukrainian guards flung open the doors and chased the people out of the wagons with their leather whips. Instructions came from a loudspeaker: 'Undress completely, including artificial limbs and spectacles. Give your valuables up at the counter. Tie your shoes together carefully.' Then women and girls were herded into a building to be shorn, and their hair put into potato sacks. Then the deportees were moved along a path to their death. Outwardly Stangl showed no compassion whatsoever. He looked on with a cold indifference as those in the procession went to their deaths, hoping probably that the gassing process would not cause any more unsettling problems. He was now supposed to bury all those killed in the gas chambers. He was aware that this was an inadequate method of body disposal, but he had no other choice. Thousands of bodies were disposed of in this manner. From the gas chamber entrance the corpses would be loaded onto a truck and driven to the pit and dumped. Powdered lime would be thrown over the bodies, which were then covered with soil.

The summer of 1942 was particular hot and dry and the buried corpses started to putrefy. The rotting bodies began rising to the surface and there was a terrible stench across the camp. Plagues of rats were seen gnawing at the corpses. The whole area was covered with swarms of flies and where the decomposed bodies had been dumped, traces of body fluids oozed out of the holes.

By the summer of 1942, both Sobibor and Belzec were running simultaneously, and despite the technical problems of machinery breaking down and the problems with body disposal the 'Reinhard' camps were achieving what they had been intended for, the mass extermination of Jews.

Whilst Sobibor and Belzec continued to operate at full capacity, a far bigger installation was being prepared, which was intended to receive all transports from Warsaw and Bialystok ghettos. The site chosen was near the small village of Treblinka in the northeastern part of the General Government. It was situated between a maze of railway lines in a dense pine forest not far from the village of Malkinia. Planners had purposely selected the area because the woods naturally concealed the camp from both the Malkinia-Kosov road to its north and the Malkinia-Siedlce railway, which ran to its west. Just to the south-west a rail line connected Treblinka station with a gravel quarry. The quarry had already been utilized by the SS for raw materials and a slave labour force had been put to work there. In the summer of 1941, the SS established a labour camp called Treblinka I, where some 1,000 Polish and Jewish detainees lived and worked. 'Labour camp Treblinka' was established by the ordinance of the Governor of the Warsaw district on 15 November 1941. The mining of gravel from the pits at Treblinka I was directed by the *SS-Sonderkommando Treblinka* (SS Special Command Treblinka). It was a lucrative enterprise conducted and headed by a German firm called the *Deutschen Herd-und Steinwerk GmbH Kieswerk Treblinka* (German hearth and masonry works, Ltd., gravel works Treblinka). It would be in the area around the quarry that the SS planned to build the new camp.

In late April 1942, an SS team arrived in the Treblinka area and toured the surrounding forests, determining where the installation would be constructed. The area certainly did nothing to inspire the small committee of SS officers, half of which had never been to Poland. The town of Treblinka with its dreary buildings and hut-like dwellings reinforced their distaste for the East. Yet, whatever malevolent thoughts they had about the apparent squalor in which the Poles lived, they knew they had come specifically to Treblinka for a serious purpose and such details were irrelevant.

The plan of the camp was almost identical to Sobibor, but with some improvements. The construction of the death camp was planned for late May or early June 1942. On 1 June 1942, The Central Construction Office of the Waffen-SS and Police in Warsaw dispatched a document confirming plans to commence construction of the new camp.

Warsaw, June 1, 1942, Koszykowa 8, Post Office Box 214
Tel. 9-21-83
Certificate no. 684

The Pole Lucjan Puchała, born on … is employed as technician at the local administrative office of Koszykowa. It is requested that the said person be allowed to pass unhindered and that he not be called in for other work. This certificate loses effect on the 15th of June 1942 and can be extended only by the local administrating office. The card is to be voluntarily returned on its expiration day.

Director of the Central Construction Office
[Signature illegible] *SS-Scharführer.*[6]

The contractors assigned to build Treblinka were the German construction firms Schönbronn of Leipzig and Schmidt-Münstermann. These firms were to receive their commissions from the Central Construction Office of the Waffen-SS and Police in Warsaw. In charge of construction was *SS-Obersturmführer* Richard Thomalla, who had completed the building contract at Sobibor and had been replaced there by Stangl in April 1942. For almost eight weeks Thomalla and his subordinates oversaw the construction of Treblinka. The bulk of the labour force was Jewish, transported there by trucks from the neighbouring villages of Wegrow and Stoczek Wegrowski. There were also a number of Poles used from the nearby labour camp Treblinka I. *SS-Untersturmführer* Heinz Auerswald from the office of the commissioner of the Warsaw ghetto supplied much of the construction materials. Thomalla also used local trade as well and obtained wood from the surrounding forests and sand and gravel from the nearby pit. A witness, Lucjan Puchala, wrote:

Initially we did not know the purpose of building the branch track, and it was only at the end of the job that I found out from conversations among Germans that the track was to lead to a camp for Jews. The work took two weeks, and it was completed on 15 June 1942. Parallel to the construction of the track, earthworks continued. The works were supervised by a German, an SS captain. At the beginning, Polish workers from the labour camp, which had already been operating in Treblinka, were used as the workforce. Subsequently, Jews from Wegrow and Stoczek Wegrowski started to be brought in by trucks. There were 2–3 trucks full of Jews that were daily brought in to the camp. The SS-men and Ukrainians supervising the work killed a few dozen people from those brought in to work every day. So that when I looked from the place where I work to the place where the Jews worked, the field was covered with corpses. The imported workers were used to dig deep ditches and to build various barracks. In particular, I know that a building was built of bricks and concrete, which, as I learned later, contained people-extermination chambers.[7]

The conditions on site under which the labour force had to work were appalling, even for the Poles. They had become slaves for the SS, and the machines they were using were death traps. Many died, and few survived without permanent injury. Malnourished, badly equipped, lacking protective gear, constantly harassed by the guards, the workers had little chance of surviving the arduous labour.

Both the SS and Ukrainian guards killed many of the Jewish workers. Jane Sulkowski recalled:

Germans killed Jews at work by shooting them or beating them to death with sticks. I saw two such cases, in which SS men, during the grubbing-out jobs, forced Jews to walk under the falling tree by which they were crushed. It also happened that SS men would often rush into the barracks where, drunk or sober, they went on shooting at the Jews who were inside.[8]

An SS orderly, who was present during the construction of the camp, saw a daily procession of dead and injured trundle past his cabin on wheelbarrows and stretchers. One day whilst aiding a colleague who was injured near a trench he witnessed the maltreatment of the workmen. A number of them were constantly beaten with sticks or truncheons, and there were hurlings into the nearby pit, shootings, and every imaginable form of torture. Those that were ill or too weak to continue working were either shot in front of the work-detail or dragged away and executed in the forest. The other workers were compelled to continue working without pause until the foreman blew his whistle ordering every man to lay down his tools. By the end of the day the majority of the men did not have the physical strength for further work. Many were on the point of collapsing, but those that had become too weak even to stand on their own two feet ran the risk the following morning of being declared unfit for further work and taken away. Those that had actually died on site from exhaustion or had been killed for some minor infringement earlier that day were piled up in heaps ready for collection by cart. Early the next morning the foreman would take stock of his workforce. Any man he deemed was no longer able to perform to the satisfaction of the SS was selected for death. The SS knew that the fear of being killed was enough to spur the workers to greater efforts and that they undertook tasks beyond their physical strength as a result of such fear. According to SS reports it is also clear that injured or ill workers regularly refrained from seeking medical treatment out of terror of being executed. The death and injury rate of the construction gangs was mainly the result of the SS physically abusing their work force. Had it not been in the summer, which was particularly hot and dry that year, the workers would have undoubtedly suffered even more trying to combat the biting cold in terrible muddy conditions. Had this been the case, the death rate would have been even higher. In spite of the hardship, the workers continued to assemble the camp, constructing the primitive, hastily thrown-together barracks and other buildings at a tremendous rate.

The site itself formed a rectangle, 600 x 400 metres, and the overall area was approximately 134,500 m² (13.45 hectares). Thomalla ordered that two sets of fences and barbed-wire obstacles should be erected first. The main footings and the construction of the brick and wood buildings would then be built.

The inner fence was nearly four metres in height. A contractor was brought in to conceal the fence with foliage and tree branches that were intertwined to hide the camp from outside view. A second fence was built about 45 metres from the first and included chains of antitank obstacles wrapped in barbed wire. Between both fences the area of land was left barren. This was done in order to ensure that no prisoners could try to hide, and would allow the guards maximum visual surveillance of the area. Fences also surrounded the area within the camp, and at each corner of the installation 8-metre high wooden watch towers were constructed.

There were a number of construction gangs given various building jobs. There were those that prepared the sandy infertile land, levelling the terrain, others laying the roads, digging basements, drainage systems, laying pipe work and wells, and then there were those brought in responsible for painting, electrical installation, heating and plumbing.

A Polish construction worker called Grzegorz Wozniak drafted in by the SS to help with plans for the drainage system wrote:

The site was built at amazing speed for its general size. I was brought to this area near the village of Treblinka to assist in the drainage of the land and to co-ordinate in piping and trenches. The Germans had a few practical problems to work out, but generally all the work went well and in the time specified. In order to assist and ensure that the work was carried out quickly and effectively gangs of workers, both Jewish and Polish, were set to work for 12 hours each day under the supervision of either SS or Ukrainian guards … When I first arrived the workers appeared in good health, but within days and weeks those that were still alive had become ill or emaciated. I was concerned by the ill-treatment of the workforce, but had been told by my Polish superiors not to question the conduct of the working practices of the SS, or we may get into serious trouble.[9]

The camp was divided into three areas: the administration and staff living area, the reception area, and extermination area. The administration and staff living and reception area of the camp was known as the 'Lower Camp', whilst the extermination area was known as the 'Upper Camp'. The buildings inside the administration and staff living area comprised a guards room near the entrance to the installation, SS living quarters, arms storeroom, gasoline pump and storerooms, garage, entrance gate to the station square, camp command and the commandant's living quarters. There were services for the SS, such as a barber, sick bay and dentist, living quarters for the domestic staff, bakery, food store and supply storeroom. There were Ukrainian living quarters, stables, a chicken coop, pig pen, living quarters for kapos, a tailor shop, shoe-repairs, carpentry shop, sick room, a prisoners' kitchen, living quarters for male prisoners and female, prisoners' laundry and tool room, locksmith, a latrine and a roll-call square.

In the reception area a concrete loading ramp was erected. Behind the ramp a large reception area was built, which would be used to bring the deportees from the trains into the camp, where they would be processed. This area was known as the 'Transport Square' (*Transportplarz*) or 'Undressing Square', and was entered through a gate. This gate is where the SS planned to separate the men from the women and children. Next to this sizable square other wooden buildings were erected, which would be used as undressing rooms for men, women and children where they would be required to relinquish their valuables and have their hair shorn. In the square the latrine was enclosed by barbed wire. South of the square was the

'Sorting Square' (*Sortierplatz*), where the deportees' clothing and belongings would be sorted and readied for shipment out of the camp back to the homeland. At one end of the square, in the south-east corner, a large hole had been dug where the SS planned to bury those victims who died in the trains en route to the camp.

In the south-eastern part of the camp was the extermination area, or 'Upper Camp'. Planners ensured that this part of the camp was completely separate from the other two parts of the installation and it was camouflaged. The total area of the 'Upper Camp' measured approximately 200 x 250 metres.

The gas chambers were erected inside the extermination area inside a huge brick building that had been built at considerable speed. In total there were three gas chambers measuring 5 x 5 metres, each 2.6 metres in height. The construction was very similar to that of the gas chambers constructed at Sobibor. Attached to the main brick building was a smaller building that contained a petrol-driven engine, which introduced carbon monoxide through pipes into the chambers. Installed next to the petrol-driven engine was a diesel-driven generator that supplied electricity to the entire camp.

The entrance doors to the gas chambers opened onto a wooden corridor along the front of the building. Each of these doors was 1.8 metres high and 0.9 metre wide. The doors closed hermetically and could be locked from outside. Inside the gas chambers, opposite each entrance door, was another large wooden door. These doors were also hermetically sealed when closed. The gas chambers' walls were covered with white tiles about two-thirds up. Shower-heads and pipes were fixed to the ceiling, designed to fool the deportees into believing they were having a shower. In fact, all the piping was intended to carry the poison gas into the chambers.

Jan Sulkowski, who was one of the bricklayers working on the gas chamber building, described the gas chambers:

> SS men said it was to be a path. Only later on, when the building was almost completed, I realized that it was to be a gas chamber. What was indicative of it was a special door of thick steel insulated with rubber, twisted with a bolt and placed in an iron frame; and also the fact that in one of the building compartments there was put an engine, from which three iron pipes led through the roof to the three remaining parts of the building … A specialist from Berlin came to put tiles inside and he told me that he had already built such a chamber elsewhere.[10]

Very near to the gas chambers an excavator had been brought in to the 'Upper Camp' from the quarry at the Treblinka penal camp, and had been used to dig a very large ditch about 50 metres long, 25 metres wide, and 10 metres in depth. This huge ditch would be used to bury the dead, and in order to transport the corpses from the gas chambers a narrow-gauge railway was laid, with trolleys pushed by prisoners. South of the gas chamber, still in the 'Upper Camp', a wooden barrack building was constructed. This building, surrounded by a fence and barbed wire and facing the gas chamber, served as living quarters for the guards in that part of the camp. There was also a guardroom and watcher tower built nearby.

The 'Upper Camp' was connected to the 'Lower Camp' by the 'tube', or as the SS in Treblinka called it, 'the road to heaven'. At the entrance to 'the road to heaven', near the women's undressing hut, a sign read: *Zur Badeanstalt*, 'To the Showers'.

By mid-June 1942 the camp was far from completed. Dr Irmfried Eberl, who was in charge of overall construction of the installation wrote a number of times to Dr Heinz Auerswald *Kommissar für den jüdischen Wohnbezirk* (commissioner for the Jewish residential district) in Warsaw appealing for the supply of more building materials from the Warsaw ghetto workshops and the items needed to complete the narrow-gauge railway and electrical installations.

In late June *SS Unterscharführer* Erich Fuchs installed a generator, which supplied electric light for the barracks. For the next few weeks Fuchs and his co-workers continued labouring night and day completing most of the electrical work in the camp.

By the end of June the finishing touches were made to the buildings of Treblinka. During early July a gang of labourers were brought into the camp to complete the killing facilities. Whilst it was believed that the gas chambers would be effective, Eberl was aware that they only had a limited capacity, dealing with some 600 people at one time. There were already concerns before it was even put into operation about how the camp would cope with a constant high influx of people. Nevertheless, people like Richard Thomalla and his planners saw that concentrating the mass killing in a remote corner of the site meant that the general running of Treblinka would not be disrupted, no matter how loudly those being gassed screamed. It would now only be a matter of weeks before Treblinka would be put to the test.

Chapter II

Under the Command of Dr Eberl
(phase one)

In July 1942, *SS-Hauptsturmführer* Richard Thomalla left Treblinka after handing over the new camp to the medical doctor, *SS-Unterscharführer* Irmfried Eberl. By mid-July his camp personnel, wearing the grey uniforms of the *Waffen-SS* but without the symbols of their native units, began arriving to take up their new post at a place known to them as 'TII'.

All concentration camps erected throughout the Reich and Poland were run brutally, and Treblinka would be no exception. The SS guards were all ordered to exhibit blind and absolute obedience and treat each prisoner with fanatical hatred. The commandants knew by perpetually drilling their SS guards to hate the prisoners, they were able to infuse them with anger and prepare them to mete out severe punishments.

Many of the new recruits that were picked for Treblinka and indeed for all the *Aktion Reinhard* camps were individually selected on the basis of their previous experience in the Euthanasia Programme. The main personnel had all been officers of T4, and all of them boasted an exceptional record. In total only 96 SS out of 400 had been chosen to run the three camps.

Some of those SS transferred to Treblinka had never worked in a concentration camp before. For these new SS recruits entering the concentration camp system for the first time it was a test of their ability to do their duty. They had learnt about enemies of the state, and been given an in-depth indoctrination in SS philosophy and racial superiority. These ideological teachings were aimed at producing men who ardently believed in the new Aryan order. The recruits had to listen to their commandant lecturing them regularly about the awfulness of the Jews. On the bulletin boards inside the SS barracks and canteen copies of the racist newspaper, *Der Stürmer* were displayed prominently. These propaganda newspapers had deliberately been pinned up in order to ferment hatred and violence against the prisoners. Many of the guards were easily susceptible to such anti-Semitic propaganda, especially the younger men. Within a few weeks of training they had learnt their trade of brutality.

The commandant of the camp invested each guard with absolute life-and-death power over all the inmates of the camp. Rule breaking among the prisoners was a crime. It was looked upon as an incitement to disobedience and each guard was given the power to hand out appalling punishments.

General physical abuse was meted out daily, and there were other more particular measures of cruelty. Prisoners were deprived of warm food for up to four days, they were subjected to long periods of solitary confinement on a diet of bread and water. To supplement these methods the commandant introduced corporal punishment into the daily routine. A prisoner would receive 25 strokes of the lash, carried out in the open on specific orders of the commandant in the presence of assembled SS guards. In order to ensure every SS officer, non-commissioned officer and SS guard was infused with the same brutal mentality as their commandant, each man routinely was to punish a prisoner with the lash without showing the slightest hesitancy or emotion, let alone remorse.

The guards were also taught to despise and hate emigrants, homosexuals and Jehovah's Witnesses. The commandant also delivered lectures about these dangerous enemies of National Socialism. But he instructed his guards to be particularly harsh to the Jews and use whatever violence necessary to keep them in check.

Whatever thoughts some of the less susceptible SS guards had on the concentration camp system, the majority were inspired by its harsh order and discipline. They were able to bury their emotions and become absorbed by the powers of camaraderie and loyalty to the SS. They saw their training in Germany and Poland as a learning curve. The crude and brutal values of the SS offered each guard a clarity and certainty. For many their first months in the concentration camp system were a chance to excel in what they deemed a career opportunity. Pitiless and callously thoughtless as to human suffering, their thirst for the SS order far outweighed any moral feelings. They had become increasingly convinced that a death camp was the most effective instrument available to destroy all elements hostile to the banner of National Socialism.

Many of the personnel that came to Treblinka had already served in other camps like Belzec and Sobibor, and therefore had an insight into the overall running of a death camp. The more ambitious learned much from their commandant and knew if they were to proceed through the ranks they had to outwardly display their conviction that all the prisoners detained inside the concentration camp system were inferior and implacable enemies of the state. They were aware that the slightest vestige of sympathy towards those in the concentration camps was regarded by the SS as intolerable. They were thus compelled to conceal any type of lingering empathy or compassion for those incarcerated. For a number of SS guards it was not just a personal crusade to rid the world of the enemies of the state, but more an ardent desire to be part of a membership of a privileged order, one fixated on command and obedience. The SS motto, *Meine Ehre Heisst Treue*, is germane here. This is usually translated as 'My Honour is Loyalty', or sometimes 'My Honour Means I am Loyal', the word *Heisst* being an antiquated word for 'is named'. This is not the same as claiming to be both honourable *and* loyal. The only definition of honour *is* loyalty. So that to act honourably does not mean to act, for example, chivalrously in battle: it simply means to obey.

Almost all of the German personnel posted to Treblinka came from the lower middle class. Their fathers were salesmen, shop workers and factory workers. The majority of them had finished primary school and then went on to attend middle and then secondary school. Those that had come directly from the euthanasia programme were mostly former nurses, farm workers, salesmen and craftsmen. The majority of them were Nazi party members in the ranks of the SS or SA. Generally, most of the personnel that were sent to Treblinka were of a similar social background and were regarded as absolutely 'ordinary' people. Most of the staff were married and held no criminal record. To them their posting to Treblinka was like any other duty, and the majority knew what to expect. After all, many of these men had been posted to places like Belzec and Sobibor, and had already bloodied their hands. A simple question of duty or not, they nevertheless kept their postings secret from their families and acquaintances whilst they were at places like Belzec. They also knew they had a choice – be posted to a death camp like Treblinka or fight on the battlefield with a military unit and risk death. Many though had opted to work at Treblinka not because they were trying to avoid military service, but simply because they were accustomed to the work. These men looked upon those tasks as their duty and performed them hiding behind the facade that they were 'only following orders.' – *Meine Ehre Heisst Treue*. In this way they were able to exhibit cruelty towards their victims and think that they would not be accountable for their actions. By blaming the system they subconsciously or consciously believed they could commit almost any crime and rid their moral conscience of any wrongdoing.

For some of the SS personnel being posted to Treblinka for the first time there was no feeling of despondency or apprehension. They arrived at their new, specially prepared quarters knowing that they had an important job to undertake.

In total there were around 20 SS men assigned to the camp, all of whom had never been at the front. The majority of the personnel were men aged between 26 and 40. A 40-year-old *SS-Unterscharführer,* Erich Fuchs, was one of a number of SS men that regarded his posting to Treblinka as particularly welcome, and certainly felt what he was doing there was right. This large-framed man had been a skilled motor mechanic and automotive foreman before the war. In the summer of 1941 he was drafted into the T4 programme and worked as Dr Eberl's driver in the gassing centres of Brandenburg and Bernburg. In early 1942 he was sent East where he was posted to Belzec and Sobibor. In July he was sent to Treblinka to install another gassing engine. To assist Fuchs was *SS-Hauptscharführer* Lorenz Hackenholt, who came to the camp to help lay the gas pipes for the gas chambers. He was a quiet-natured man, but blindly loyal and was an efficient death coordinator who had also helped build and operate the gas chambers at Belzec and Sobibor.

Another SS man that arrived early that summer was *SS-Hauptscharführer* Alfons Lindenmuller. He had been attached to a Waffen-SS detachment prior to his new appointment to Treblinka, but had never served in a concentration camp before. Prior to his posting he had been sent to the Trawniki training camp where he received his concentration camp training. Driving towards Treblinka along the sandy roads on his first day Lindenmuller passed several information boards, with notices prohibiting anyone from entering the forest. The boards warned that anyone who entered the forest would be shot on sight by the guards patrolling the area. Approaching the gates to the camp he was surprised that it appeared anything but forbidding. The road leading into the installation, the barracks, commandant's house, the ammunition depot, the garage and petrol station was all banked with beautiful flowers. Once inside the camp he had to report to the administration office, and from there was allocated a bunk in the SS barracks. Those he met in the SS quarters were friendly and welcoming and he was immediately asked if he had eaten anything. He was surprised that in addition to the basic SS rations of bread and sausage there was many other items of food available. Alcohol too was abundant, especially Polish vodka. The living quarters were very comfortable, and he was astonished to see females walking around. He later learnt that the cleaning of the SS quarters was done by Jewish girls, the cooking however, by Polish non-Jewish women. There were three Polish girls working in the German mess, and they lived there too. Strange though it may seem, they had days off and could go and see their families in the surrounding villages.

He was also surprised to see that the commandant had organized a musical trio, which would often play for the SS personnel during meals, in the evenings, and at parties. Three Jews that could play musical instruments were brought to the commandant's quarters where Eberl asked them to play for the SS.

For Lindmuller and other personnel another enticing aspect of working in the death camp was the salary. The official monthly wage was 58 *Reich Marks*, but for each day in the camp they received a bonus of 18 *Reich Marks*. With the month's pay together with bonuses this amounted to some 600 *Reich Marks*. Additionally, the right to at least three weeks leave every three months made the job very attractive to someone like Lindenmuller. Yet the contrast between his comfortable life in the SS and the brutal existence of the regime would certainly test his conscience in the weeks and months to come. Whilst coming from a military background he was fully aware of the job he was about to undertake. He found most of his comrades were veteran concentration camp personnel. A number of them had already used their own initiative to help devise methods by which to kill large numbers of people. Whilst sitting with them in the mess they spoke openly and without emotion about the killing of men, women, and children. They saw Treblinka as a new enterprise, a specialized death camp that they hoped would bring bigger and better results than any other camp in the system. These SS men were determined to carry on their orgy of destruction. Lindenmuller was aware that his job was secret and that none of his relatives, friends or loved ones were to be told anything about it. Almost every SS man that came to Treblinka was determined from the outset to conceal as much of the gruesome truth as possible from the outside world.

As a rank-and-file member of the SS, Lindenmuller had decided to come to Treblinka not because he was ordered to but because he believed in the overall Nazi vision. Like so many of his comrades he could have at any time chosen to leave and be posted to the front, but he stayed.

These men were bribed by other special inducements, such as extra rations of cigarettes, schnapps and sausage. Some, however, needed no urging to bloody their hands, and went about killing and abusing their victims with enthusiasm.

As in any industrial operation, their superiors were well aware that such mass murder could only be achieved if the trains sent people on schedule, if the gas chambers worked in synchronization with each other and could cope with the vast numbers of new arrivals. Already chaos had ensued at Belzec because it did not have gas chambers big or numerous enough to deal with the huge numbers of people arriving daily. The problem had become so bad that in June 1942 the camp shut down for a month and new gas chambers were hastily built. At Sobibor, the problem was both the size of the gas chambers and transportation by rail to the camp. Much now depended on Treblinka to ease the burden placed on the 'Reinhard' camps.

Dr Eberl was well aware what was demanded of him by his superiors in Berlin. He was determined to deliver them an exceptional killing rate that far outweighed that of any other camp in the Nazi empire. A crucial part of the killing process was undoubtedly the delivery of the Jews. This factory had to be fed with massive numbers. Even as the last touches were being made to the gas chambers at Treblinka Eberl received confirmation that a whole series of resettlement 'actions' were being conducted right across occupied Poland. These actions saw the vast majority of Jews now being sent directly to Belzec and Sobibor.

On 22 July 1942, Treblinka railway station received a telegram outlining that trains would start travelling between Warsaw and Treblinka. It confirmed that the trains would have 60 closed cars each, and that they would be transporting deportees from the Warsaw ghetto. They would be unloaded and then sent back empty.

The clearing of the Warsaw ghetto and the organizing of the transportation of the Jews to the death camps within Poland was an immense undertaking. The responsibility for the shipments from Warsaw in liaison with the railway authorities of the *Ostbahn*, was left in the capable of hands of *SS-Hauptsturmführer* Hermann Höfle, Globocnik's chief of staff. He was quite aware that this was the largest operation of this kind thus far. The first and major phase of this operation was set in motion on 22 July 1942. All of the inhabitants were destined for the new death camp, code-named TII. On 22 July Höfle issued the following order to the Jewish Council in Warsaw:

The Jewish Council is hereby informed of the following:

1. All Jewish persons irrespective of age or sex who live in Warsaw will be resettled in the east.
2. The following are excluded from the resettlement:
(a) All Jewish persons who are employed by the German authorities or by German agencies and can provide proof of it.
(b) All Jewish persons who belong to the Jewish Council and are employees of the Jewish Council.
(c) All Jewish persons who are employed by German firms and can provide proof of it.
(d) All Jews capable of work who have not hitherto been employed. They are to be placed in barracks in the ghetto.
(e) All Jewish persons who are members of the personnel of the Jewish hospitals. Similarly, the members of the Jewish disinfection troops.
(f) All Jewish persons who belong to the Jewish police force.
(g) All Jewish persons who are close relatives of the persons referred to in (a)-(f). Such relatives are restricted to wives and children.
(h) All Jewish persons who on the first day of the resettlement are in one of the Jewish hospitals and are not capable of being released. The fitness for release will be decided by a doctor to be designated by the Jewish Council.
3. Every Jewish person being resettled may take 15kg of his property as personal luggage. All valuables may be taken: gold, jewellery, cash etc. Food for three days should be taken.
4. The resettlement begins on 22 July 1942 at 11 o'clock …

II. The Jewish Council is responsible for providing the daily quota of Jews for transportation. To carry out this task the Jewish council will use the Jewish police force (100 men). The Jewish Council will ensure that every day from 22 July onwards, by 16.00 at the latest, 6,000 Jews will be assembled directly on the loading platform near the transfer office. To start with, the Jewish Council may take the quotas of Jews from the whole population. Later, the Jewish Council will receive special instructions according to which particular streets and blocks of flats are to be cleared …

VIII. Punishments:
(a) Any Jewish person who leaves the ghetto at the start of the resettlement without belonging to the categories of persons outlined in 2(a) and (c), and in so far as they were not hitherto entitled to do so, will be shot.
(b) Any Jewish person who undertakes an act which is calculated to evade or disturb the resettlement measures will be shot.
(c) Any Jewish person who assists in an act calculated to evade of disturb the resettlement measures will be shot.
(d) All Jews who, on completion of the resettlement are encountered in Warsaw and do not belong to the categories referred to in 2(a)-(h) will be shot.

The Jewish council is hereby informed that, in the event that the orders and instructions are not carried out 100%, an appropriate number of the hostages who have been taken in the meantime will be shot.[11]

The first transport of Jews from the Warsaw ghetto left Malkinia for Treblinka in the early morning of 23 July. Eberl instructed his SS personnel and Ukrainian guards to prepare for their first arrivals. A large notice at the entrance of the camp was also erected. It read:

Attention Warsaw Jews!
You are now entering a transit camp from which you will be transported to a labour camp.
To prevent epidemics both clothing and luggage must be handed in for disinfecting.

Gold, cash, foreign exchange, and jewellery are to be given up at the cash desk in return for a receipt. They will be later returned on presentation of the receipt.

All those arriving must cleanse themselves by taking a bath before continuing their journey.

SS-Unterscharführer Lothar Boelitz and *SS-Unterscharführer* Ernst Gentz were the SS men to receive the first batch of Warsaw deportees on the platform. They, like everyone else in the camp, had explicit instructions from the commandant that the process from unloading to murder had to be undertaken at rapid speed. Rudolf Emmerich and Willi Klinzmann were in charge of overseeing the shunting of the trains. A Pole, Franciszek Zabecki, who was working at the camp described the scene:

Four SS men from the new camp were waiting. They had arrived earlier by car and asked us how far from Treblinka the 'special train with deportees' was. They had already received word of the trains departure from Warsaw ... A smaller engine was already at the station, waiting to bring a section of the freight cars into the camp. Everything was planned and prepared in advance.[12]

The first train of some sixty closed freight cars crossed the Bug River outside Treblinka during the morning of 23 July. Ukrainian guards that were outside the station announced its approach by firing a volley of rifle shots into the air. The train squealed to a halt, and Emmerich and Klinzmann divided the train into three sections; each section was shunted separately into the camp. Franciszek Zabecki recalled:

The train was made up of sixty closed cars, crowded with people. These included the young and elderly, men and women, children and babies. The car doors were locked from outside and the air apertures barred with barbed wire. On the car steps on both sides of the car and on the roof, a dozen or so SS soldiers [there would have been Ukrainian guards too] stood or lay with machine guns at the ready. It was hot, and most people in the freight cars were in a faint ... As the train approached, an evil spirit seemed to take hold of the SS men who were waiting. They drew their pistols, returned them to their holsters, and whipped them out again, as if

45

they wanted to shoot and kill. They came near the freight cars and tried
to calm the noise and weeping; then they started yelling and cursing the
Jews, all the while calling to the train workers, 'tempo, fast!' Then they
returned to the camp to receive the deportees.[13]

The SS employed terror and speed as a means of ensuring a smooth
processing of the Jews. A Jewish survivor later recalled the scene:

When the train arrived in Treblinka I can remember seeing great piles
of clothing. Now we feared that the rumours really had been true.
I remember saying to my wife more or less: this is the end. We were
transported in goods wagons. The goods wagons were very overcrowded.
We were able to take something to eat with us but got nothing to drink
and that was the worst thing. When the train arrived in Treblinka a
considerable number of people had already died of exhaustion. I can no
longer remember how many there were. I would like to point out that
one of the worst things about the transport was the lack of air. There was
only a small window covered with a grille and there were no sanitary
facilities. Anybody can imagine what that meant.

I can remember the terrible confusion when the doors were pulled
open in Treblinka. The SS and Ukrainians shouted 'get out, out'. The
members of the so-called Red Jewish *Kommando* also shouted and
yelled. Then the people who had arrived began to scream and complain.
I remember too that whips were used on us. Then, we were told: 'Men to
the right, women to the left and get undressed.' My little daughter was
with me and then ran to her mother when we were separated. I never saw
them again and could not even say good-bye. Then while I was undressing
I was selected by a German to be a so-called work-Jew.[14]

As the deportees were unloaded off the freight cars Ukrainian guards took
up their positions around the reception area and on the surrounding roofs,
whilst another group of well-armed Ukrainians and SS took up position
on the platform. At the unloading ramp there were a group of prisoners
nicknamed 'Blue' *Kommandos*. They were given the task of carrying all
clothes to the square adjacent to the ramp, and clearing the wagons of
the deportees including those that had died en route. Once everyone
was removed the cars were hastily hosed down with water. After they had

been cleaned the switching engine driver coupled the cars and shunted the empty carriages out of the camp in order to make room for the next delivery of cars.

On the ramp there was a hive of activity as the newcomers were crammed together. Most of them did not suspect the truth. Many believed that they had simply arrived at a quiet provincial railway. As they stood assembled waiting for instruction, Eberl came through the gate flanked by his deputy *SS-Rottenführer* Max Biala, and spoke to them. He told them calmly that they would soon be sent on their way further east, but had stopped at Treblinka because of their appalling hygienic conditions. They were required first to be disinfected, but prior to this he asked that they kindly left their luggage on the ramp and handed in all money and valuables they had. Everybody, he said, was to get a towel and soap, and he reminded them not to forget their deposit receipt. The speech was welcomed by those exhausted after spending hours crammed inside the freight cars.

For Eberl and his subordinates this was the easiest and most practical means to deceive the Jews and murder them as quickly as possible. Each member of the camp was trained to dupe all new arrivals into believing they had alighted at a disinfecting stop where they would be treated as a precaution against disease. They were then to be hurried through the camp to their deaths as quickly as possible. Eberl had been told by his superiors that the key to successful mass murder on a grand scale was to conduct the whole process in an atmosphere of great calm. Initially, this is exactly what happened. Whilst he spoke to the newcomers his deputy or one of his other subordinates kept a careful watch over individuals who were thought likely to cause trouble. At the tiniest sign of an attempt to disrupt the process, such people were discreetly moved away, taken out of view, and shot with a small-calibre pistol.

Whilst Eberl concluded his short speech other SS officers selected a handful of skilled workers and strong young men from the transport. In order not to raise any suspicion among the new arrivals those that were selected for work detail were marched quietly off out of the square through a side gate. Those that remained on the square had been selected to be processed for the gas chambers. Men and women were separated, and the women were ordered to the barracks on the left, nicknamed by the SS the 'Beauty Salon'. Inside they undressed and their hair was shorn. The men undressed outside on the square and were ordered to fold their clothes and tie their shoelaces. A group of Polish prisoners nicknamed 'Red' *Kommandos* helped the new arrivals undress and pacified them prior to leading them to the 'road to heaven'.

SS-Unterscharführer Franz Suchomel supervised the female undressing barrack and led the victims through the 'tube' to the gas chambers. He took his duties very seriously and was generally well liked among his comrades. Before the war he had been a tailor, and in 1940 began working in the T4 euthanasia programme photographic section in Berlin and Hadamar prior to his posting to Treblinka. He was a quiet and sentimental individual, hardworking and enjoyed being surrounded by family and friends. His family was never anti-Semitic and remarks against the Jews were unknown in his house. Yet, when he entered the world of the SS his views changed and became an ardent believer in the Nazi vision. Whatever his thoughts and beliefs, nothing prepared him for Treblinka. It was a shock even to an SS man like Suchomel. Nonetheless, the Nazi decree that the Jews were to be exterminated was in his mind binding. The thought of actually refusing an order, regardless of what it was, never ever entered his head. Like so many of his comrades he knew that in order to embark on his murderous career all consciousness of individual guilt had to be eliminated. Being subjected constantly to camp life cauterised his conscience. Some of his comrades regularly watched the shipments arrive and became morbidly fascinated by the spectacle. They witnessed the selection process at the unloading ramps and saw firsthand the awful scenes of families being torn apart. They saw the emotional torment of mothers who suspected what was about to happen to them, as they walked with their children to their deaths. The majority were seen clinging to their offspring trying to conceal their emotion so that it did not trouble or upset their children.

Outwardly the SS men showed no compassion. Perhaps the killing by gas was easier to deal with psychologically than murdering men, women and children face-to-face. Instead of such drama and close violence, they could be processed like cattle and sent into a building and quietly killed in a remote part of the camp. For most of the SS this meant that that their daily routine would only be punctuated by the constant flow of deportees into the camp, and the preparation for their murder – not the deaths themselves.

Treblinka had begun to operate; those running the camp in late July and early August could not have known the magnitude of the horror that would soon unfold there.

The final stage of the process at Treblinka saw the naked Jews being directed towards the entrance of the 'road to the heaven', which had high fences on both sides and a white gravel path. On either side of the fence stood SS and Ukrainian guards with dogs. Intermingled with the awful sounds of barking and growling dogs, the guard's hurled abuse at the frightened and bewildered men, women and children as they ran by with their hands up. To speed up the stream of naked bodies the guards whipped and beat anyone that showed any signs of reluctance to enter the 'tube'. The so-called 'master of the bath' or *Bademaster*, continually shouted to keep the lines moving. As they were being led naked to the 'tube' Eberl ordered his little musical trio to play in a pathetic attempt to drown out the screams and calm the victims.

At the end of the gravel path stood the gas chamber. At the entrance two Ukrainian guards greeted the Jews. They were then led in file into the chamber where they could see that from the ceiling hung 'sieves' mounted on pieces of wood or metal, which appeared to be shower heads. Once crammed inside, the airtight door to the room with latch bars was shut and screwed tight. Special pumps were switched on and this began sucking out the air. With the lack of air and with everyone tightly packed together, some people began fainting. Others panicked and screamed. The noise was soon drowned out by the throb of an engine. From the pipes over their heads, dark, asphyxiating smoke began to appear. This created even more panic inside the chamber and often led to people trying to break down the door. Children and mothers could be heard crying. Some of the hundreds of human beings struggling desperately for their lives managed to stay conscious for 30 or even 40 minutes. Gradually, the noise faded away altogether. One SS man put his ear to the door and listened. Once he was certain everyone inside had been successfully gassed he signalled for a *kommando* of diggers to open the door. The gas-tight door was then unbolted and opened, and the task of extracting the dead women, children and old people was begun by the 'diggers' once they were sure that all the victims were no longer moving and that the poisoned air was no longer hazardous. Many of the dead still had their eyes open and were hanging onto one another. Some bodies were crushed by the door, whilst others were found lying around. Many had tried to escape, making their way in panic to the doorway. Their bodies were covered with scratches and bruises as the victims trampled one another in a frantic effort to escape the gas.

Many had blood oozing from their noses and mouths with their faces bloated and blue, and some were so deformed they were unrecognizable. Inside the chamber it was very hot and some, in particular the children, probably died of suffocation before the gassing. In many cases mothers were still clinging to their offspring and their limbs had to be prised apart. Some bodies were covered in urine, excrement or vomit.

The diggers either dragged or wheeled the corpses out to a location adjacent to the building overlooking the gas chambers. A *kommando*, known as the 'dentist', inspected the corpses for dentures or gold teeth and then began extracting them by means of a chisel or hammer. Any gold found in the victim's mouths was placed in a jar containing acid. The 'dentist' was also given the task of searching other body cavities for smuggled valuables using pliers and a chisel. Once he confirmed that the gassed and now mutilated corpse was 'clean', the body was returned to the diggers. The diggers then dragged the victims to a special wagon that sat on rails, which transported the murdered victims to the pit a few metres away. Under the supervision of two SS men the diggers then emptied the wagon into the pit. Once the pit was full, they covered the corpses with lime first, and then soil.

Whilst the prisoners threw the bodies in the huge pit the SS men watched, constantly drinking vodka, cognac and other alcohol. To be able to freely beat and brutalize the prisoners was one thing. But there were those that struggled with the actual sight of mass extermination. So alcohol was a remedy that was universally used at Treblinka among the SS. Overall though, the burying of the corpses did not cause the SS any recorded or witnessed emotional disturbance.

Within the first weeks of August 1942, Eberl's mounting workload had become immense, and he could see no end to the constant flow of detainees arriving at the camp. Yet, despite the growing demands placed on him, these were overridden by his burning desire to outshine any other death camp in the Nazi empire. His thirst to hold the title of administrator of the largest killing centre in the Reich outweighed any worries he had about how he would achieve it. For him only the numbers of dead mattered, and he ardently believed that his bosses in Berlin were in accord.

During a meeting with his deputy Biala, Eberl calculated that within 90 minutes of an arrival of deportees around 2,000 could be processed and disposed of in the pits. On paper the plans seemed attainable, but the numbers arriving were too high. Within a couple of weeks Treblinka was in chaos.

There were so many shipments to the camp that Eberl and his staff could no longer cope with the disembarkation and gassing process. So, instead of prioritizing and trying to maintain an efficient system, Eberl decided to speed the killings by not only having the shipments gassed, but killed by shooting as well. Whilst this was far from an acceptable method of large scale murder, Eberl was determined to try and overcome the chaos and disorder by killing his way out of the situation in this way. What followed in the last sweltering weeks of August 1942 was an orgy of death and destruction unheard of in any other camp. Both the SS and their Ukrainian counterparts unleashed terrible brutality upon those that entered the camp. Initially, disembarkation was undertaken in relative calm with the majority of the victims not knowing what was going to happen to them. However, within a couple of weeks those that disembarked witnessed horrible sights. Hundreds of bodies were lying all around. Piles of bundles and clothes were strewn everywhere, all mixed together. SS soldiers and Ukrainian guards that were standing on the roofs of barracks often fired indiscriminately into the crowd, which frequently caused widespread panic and further disorder. Even during the train journey into Treblinka corpses lined the railway line. As the train got nearer, more dead littered the way. The agony of the Jews did not begin at Treblinka; but when they boarded the train bound for the camp. Furthermore, because the gas chambers were not sufficient to deal with the numbers of people scheduled to be killed, there was a bottleneck of trains waiting to go through, and as a result some trains were queuing seven miles away.

Debarkation at Treblinka became so chaotic and disorganized that Eberl could no longer cope. He was particularly scathing towards his subordinates and as a result of the deteriorating situation encouraged his men to commit bestial acts. The SS and Ukrainian guards were ordered to work as fast as possible to move the new arrivals through and have them murdered at whatever cost. The pressure was so enormous that guards who had shown some degree of restraint towards the deportees were now observed whipping Jewish woman and children and actually chasing them into the gas chambers. They murdered Jews with their own hands and shot dead anyone that would not move quickly enough.

SS-Scharführer Heinrich Artur Matthes, who was appointed chief officer commanding Camp II and the gas chambers as well as killer at the *Lazarett*, where the Ukrainians called him 'doctor', was regarded as a loathsome man, even by some of the cruellest guards. Red faced and sweating, he would often be seen screaming obscenities and beating Jews. Out near the pits one day he shot a 'digger' called Ilik Weintraub because he was not transferring the bodies from the gas chambers to the pits quickly enough. Jerzy Rajgrodzki, a prisoner in the extermination area, recalled that

> ... he used to beat the prisoners with a completely expressionless, apathetic look on his face, as if the beatings were part of his daily routine. He always saw to it that the roll-call area would always be extremely clean. One of the prisoners had to rake the sand in the square all day long, and he had to do it with Prussian exactness.[15]

SS-Unterscharführer Mentz Willi was another notorious SS man at Treblinka who did not need any encouragement from Eberl to commit terrible acts of cruelty. He was assigned first to Camp II and later to Camp I as chief of the *Landwirtschaftskommando* (Agricultural Command). According to Wirth, Willi was an intelligent, hard-working and determined individual who had demonstrated his effectiveness within the SS. Prior to the war he was an unskilled worker in a sawmill and he had achieved nothing except for passing a master milkman's examination. In 1940 he began taking cows and pigs to Grafeneck euthanasia centre and from 1941 to early summer 1942 worked in the gardens of Hadamar.

In the early summer Willi was offered a posting to a concentration camp. He appeared to be attracted by the nature of the duty involved, in spite of the fact that he did not know what was actually in store for him. Once he was in training the prestige of the uniform, elitism, 'toughness' and comradeship soon outweighed any moral scruples. He enjoyed meting out harsh and often brutal punishments for the slightest infractions of camp rules. For Willi, Treblinka had given him a chance to excel when previously in life he had failed. Whilst on duty he roamed the camp in an arrogant manner and would be seen beating, kicking, slapping and whipping prisoners ruthlessly. He seemed to take great pride in the fact that his mere presence caused the inmates to tremble with fear. He gleefully followed the policy of directed and disciplined terror laid down during his guard training. This barbarous man could conduct his cruel beatings with a nonchalant and cavalier attitude. At the pits he regularly forced groups of prisoners to watch the dead being thrown into the pits, before he personally shot each one of them in the back of the neck. According to one of his comrades he was remembered as being unkempt and dishevelled with a black moustache. But what he was most remembered for was routine shootings that took place in the 'Infirmary' as the transports arrived. A prisoner named Richard Glazar recalled, 'He shoots and shoots, and keeps shooting, sometimes moving on to the next target even when the previous shot had not found its mark and a sentient victim simply slipped into the fires. Messy work.'[16]

Before Willi arrived at Treblinka he showed no signs of sadism; by all accounts he lived a modest life in a relatively loving family environment. It was the circumstances of Treblinka, probably through the influence of Eberl's brutal reign, that brought forth the Willi the victims would come to fear and hate – a grim reminder of how hard it is to predict who, in exceptional situations, will become a monster.

Another SS man who was able freely to perform cruel acts against the Jews that August was *SS-Stabsscharführer* Otto Stadie. This large, balding 45-year-old man, originally from Berlin, was nicknamed by the Jews '*Fesele*' (Yiddish for Barrel). Before the war he worked as a male nurse at the clinic for the mentally ill, *Heil -und Pflegeanstalt* in Berlin. Afterwards he became an ambulance sergeant in an engineer-infantry-company. In 1941 he was posted to the Bernberg euthanasia killing site before getting a posting to Treblinka. When he first arrived he became company commander of the Ukrainian guard unit. He was also part of the SS squad who received prisoners with clubs and whips on the platform when deportations arrived. It did not take him long before he was slaking an unquenchable thirst for brutality on the new arrivals. Anyone he found with smuggled valuables in their possession was either beaten or shot on the spot in full view of other deportees. He was known among some of his comrades as an arrogant, self-righteous individual with no morals or scruples. He would arrive back at the barracks late every evening exhausted, and because of his warped sensibilities would make no effort to hide and would even boast of his hideous acts of brutality against the Jews earlier that day.

The overwhelming majority of the SS men in Treblinka perpetrated many acts of inhuman torture and cruelty on the Jews that summer. Yet, in the chaotic disorder of the camp there were a few SS men that never felt compelled to display extreme acts of brutality and blood lust. *SS-Unterscharführer* Erwin Herman Lambert, for instance, was one SS man that did show a degree of humane behaviour towards the prisoners. This

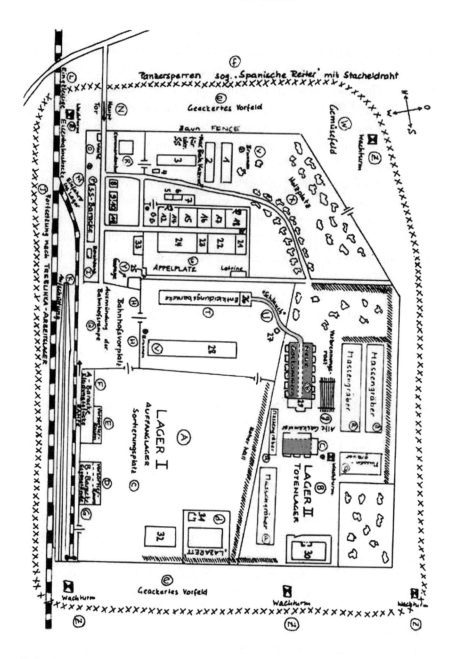

GLAZAR MAP

Richard Glazar was a member of the camouflage commando with a keen eye for detail. His map contains some discrepancies in the placing of features as well as the overall shape of the camp. The extermination site ('Upper Camp') was not known to him and his sketch of it is therefore not reliable. (Courtesy of ARC)

33-year-old, originally from Schildow near Berlin, was a former mason. In 1940 he was assigned to installing the gas chambers at the euthanasia institutes of Hartheim, Sonnenstein, Bernburg and Hadamar. In June 1942 he was ordered to Lublin for bricklaying assignments and was then sent to Treblinka, responsible for construction of the barracks. Together with Thomalla he was in charge of a group of builders who completed the gas chambers in August 1942. According to a prisoner named Wiernik:

> *Unterscharführer* Herman was humane and likeable. He understood us and was considerate of us. When he first entered Camp II and saw the piles [of bodies] that had been suffocated by the gas, he was stunned. He turned pale and a frightened look of suffering fell over his face. He quickly took me from the place so as not to see what was going on. With regard to us, the workers, he treated us very well. Frequently he would bring us food on the side from the German kitchen. In his eyes one could see his good-heartedness … but he feared his friends. All his deeds and movements expressed his gentle soul.[17]

Joe Siedlecki later testified about another SS man in Treblinka who treated Jewish prisoners humanely:

> There was an SS man, Karl Ludwig [*Scharführer*]. He was a good man. If I would meet him today, I would give him everything he might need. I cannot even count the times he brought me all kinds of things and helped me, or the number of people he saved.[18]

Despite this evidence of a more restrained approach towards the inmates, there were many more SS guards that came to Treblinka to prove that they could be evil and carry out their duties loyally and unquestioningly. Eberl's personnel exhibited cruelty towards their victims to such an extent that many of them actually contributed their own ideas and innovations for various forms of torture.

From the moment the SS personnel arrived in camp they inflicted pain and hardship on the new arrivals. The chaos that ensued only generated further animosity and hatred towards the Jews, and this subsequently dramatically increased the death rate in the camp. Eberl could boast that from between the end of July to the last days of August an estimated 300,000 people were murdered at Treblinka. This was a phenomenal figure, a killing rate of around 10,000 a day. To Eberl's satisfaction it was a death toll that no other camp commandant had even approached thus far.

The killing rate was looked upon as such an exceptional figure within the concentration camp system that *SS-Obersturmbannführer* Rudolf Höss, commandant of Auschwitz concentration camp in south-western Poland, had been requested by *SS-Obersturmbannführer* Adolf Eichmann to visit the death camp. He told the Auschwitz commandant that in order to prepare for the mass extermination facilities at Auschwitz, Höss should journey to a recently built concentration camp codenamed 'TII' to see for himself a fully operational death camp. The destination was kept secret from his staff, and only during his journey was Höss properly briefed on the installation and its exact location. Approaching the camp Höss could smell it from miles away. Upon Höss's arrival he met Eberl and his deputy and together they toured the area. Höss was told that the camp was divided into three parts, the first included a reception area, an area that contained housing for German staff, the guard unit, administrative offices, a clinic, storerooms, and one workshop. The second was enclosed by barbed wire fencing, which housed Jewish inmates that had been selected from incoming transports. The third area, which was the main reason for his visit, was the killing facility at the camp. Since its conception, Höss was informed that in accordance with *Aktion Reinhard*, Treblinka had been murdering around 6,000 people each day. By the time he arrived that figure had more or less doubled. Although the figures were impressive and the Commandant clearly wanted to reach the highest possible numbers to exceed all other camps, it appeared to Höss that the camp could not adequately cope with the numbers of transports. At the gas chambers where Höss was supposed to seek inspiration he observed the killing process and was not very impressed. He wrote:

> Small gas chambers were used, equipped with pipes to induce the exhaust gas from the engines, coming from old captured transport vehicles and tanks, that very often failed to work. Because of that the intakes could not be dealt with according to the plan, which was meant to clear the Warsaw ghetto. According to the camp commandant of Treblinka 80,000 people have been gassed in the course of half a year.[19]

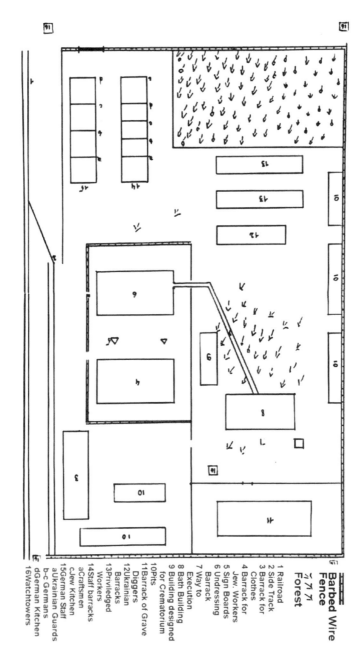

KRZEPICKI MAP

Jakub Abraham Krzepicki was deported to Treblinka on 25 August 1942. Eighteen days later he would escape, hiding himself amongst clothes that were sent back to Lublin in a freight car. (Courtesy of ARC)

In Höss's view Treblinka was not a very efficient camp. The Auschwitz gas chambers were much larger, and unlike at Treblinka he would not waste valuable resources and time killing Jews with exhaust gas. Initially, the victims that arrived at Treblinka did not know their fate, but by the time Höss had arrived there were hundreds of bodies lying everywhere decomposing. Across the square there were thousands of pieces of clothing, valuables and currency. Strewn among these personal artifacts were many dead, either killed once they arrived or who had died en route and had been dragged out of the freight car waiting for disposal. Many people too were shot in the Lower Camp, and as Höss noted, all of this of course ruined the deception that was the basis of the camp's operation – that it was a disinfecting station. As soon as they witnessed the killing or the dead lying on the ground, none believed it.

To make matters worse the three gas chambers kept breaking down and this subsequently caused a massive bottleneck of deportees. The problem had become so bad in the second week of August Eberl ordered that each transport had to be shot in the reception area. The work load for the Ukrainian and SS personnel was immense and additional ammunition was brought to the camp to cope. Because of the huge flood of transports many more prisoners were required to be selected for work detail to bury the thousands of people that were shot. Eberl ordered more burial pits to be dug, and this was done by the scoop-shovel. But since there were some seven shipments arriving daily at the camp, still more and more corpses were left unburied. The problems multiplied when the storehouse barrack designed for victim's belongings became full. The crisis was so bad that the male undressing barrack was hastily converted into a store room to cope with the belongings. Soon, piles of clothes and valuables were strewn everywhere. Every new transport added to the confusion.

Eberl's heavy drinking did not help. One night, *SS-Unterscharführer* Franz Suchomel remembered, Eberl got drunk and made a Jewish dancer dance naked in the kitchen. He ordered her to undress.

With a gradual breakdown in overall command coupled with the chaotic disorder of the camp, freight cars were now ordered to halt and wait, sometimes for 48 hours, before the human cargo could be processed. The result was a higher death toll in the freight cars themselves. Whilst this appeared to help Eberl, it actually delayed the turnaround time of the trains. The dead bodies had to be removed by hand and transported directly to the pits. There were so many bodies to bury that frequently those that had been extracted from the cars were laid out on the ramp or in the square, sometimes for days, waiting to be buried.

Another problem was that the operators of the gas chambers often did not know how long their victims should be left in the chamber until they suffocated. There were a number of instances where the gas chamber doors were opened and the victims were still alive. The doors then had to be shut again. With constant use and lack of servicing the engines that produced and fed the gas into the chambers frequently broke down causing a halt to the extermination process. Breakdowns of this nature occurred when naked men, women and children were waiting to enter the gas chamber building. When this occurred, on strict orders from Eberl, the whole transport had to be herded together immediately and shot. This of course revealed the true purpose of Treblinka to the new arrivals and caused panic and terror amongst everyone. Screaming and crying young mothers holding onto their offspring pleaded with the Ukrainian firing squad to spare the lives of their children. The Ukrainian guards killed everyone.

If this was not bad enough, engine breakdowns also occurred when the victims were already inside the chamber being gassed. Sometimes for hours, packed naked into the chamber, men, women and children had to wait until the engines had been repaired. From outside the building the guards could hear the crying and screaming and banging on the gas chamber door, begging for it to be opened.

Then, disposal: not only were the pits already overflowing with the dead, but their removal and transport in trolleys was too slow, which consequently delayed the arrival of new victims to the gas chambers. The hand-push trolley used to transport the corpses to the pits would often derail or turn over, and it was finally decided to dispense with the trolley. Instead, the prisoners had to either drag or carry the murdered victims to the pits. The process was difficult and time consuming. If a prisoner did not transport a corpse to the pit quick enough he was often beaten or shot.

Throughout the camp there was death and total disorder. A number of the SS personnel and the Ukrainians were spiralling out of control, stealing whatever they could find from the dead. Corruption at Treblinka had become widespread. The policy of the concentration camp authorities and throughout the Nazi state was absolutely clear – all valuables taken from new arrivals were the property of the Reich. But the temptation for the SS and Ukrainian guards was irresistible. Stealing was an everyday occurrence. With so much wealth flooding into the camp and with little supervision, there were so many casual opportunities to steal. The SS did most of the thieving. Even Eberl himself was looting from the pockets of the dead. Both he and his subordinates were stealing jewelry and cash in order to buy goods on the flourishing black market or as a nest egg.

However, it did not take long before information leaked to Globocnik that large sums of victims' money and valuables were disappearing into the camp staff's pockets. In fact, reports indicated that Eberl was actually sending large amounts of money to his superiors in the euthanasia programme, at Hitler's chancellery in Berlin. Globocnik immediately intervened and handed the report to Wirth.

In the last week of August Globocnik and Wirth visited Treblinka. *SS-Oberscharführer* Josef Oberhauser, Wirth's assistant, who accompanied him to Treblinka, wrote:

> In Treblinka everything was in a state of collapse. The camp was overstocked. Outside the camp, a train with deportees was unable to be unloaded as there was simply no more room. Many corpses of Jews were lying inside the camp. These corpses were already bloated. Particularly I can remember seeing many corpses in the vicinity of the fence. These people were shot from the guard towers. I heard then in Treblinka how Globocnik and Wirth summed up the following: Wirth would remain in Treblinka for the time being. Dr Eberl would be dismissed immediately. In his place, Stangl would come to Treblinka from Sobibor as commander. Globocnik said in this conversation that if Dr Eberl were not his fellow countryman, he would arrest him and bring him before an SS and police court.[20]

Stangl was relieved to be leaving Sobibor, and his departure to Treblinka was arranged whilst Sobibor was shut down for repairs to the rail line connecting the camp.

> I drove there, with an SS driver. We could smell it kilometres away. The road ran alongside the railway. When we were about fifteen, twenty minutes' drive from Treblinka, we began to see corpses by the line, first just two or three, then more, and we drove into Treblinka station, there

were what looked like hundreds of them – just lying there – they'd obviously been there for days, in the heat. In the station was a train full of Jews, some dead, some still alive ... that too, looked as if it had been there for days ... When I entered the camp and got out of the car on the square I stepped knee-deep into money; I didn't know which way to turn, where to go. I waded in notes, currency, precious stones, jewelry, and clothes. They were everywhere, decomposing, putrefying. Across the square, in the woods, just a few hundred yards away on the other side of the barbed-wire fence and all around the perimeter of the camp, there were tents and open fires with groups of Ukrainian guards and girls – whores, I found out later, from all over the countryside – weaving drunk, dancing, singing, playing music ...[21]

Stangl was greeted by Wirth who then proceeded to show him around the camp. Stangl was appalled by the chaos and was even more perturbed that the SS personnel and Ukrainian guards had been allowed to shoot at will, wherever they liked, even in front of new arrivals. Later that day Stangl left Treblinka bound for Warsaw, where he met with Globocnik to discuss Treblinka. The following day both men returned to the camp. As soon as they arrived they held a long meeting with Wirth and then afterwards went to the mess for some coffee and talked to some officers. The SS men spoke about looting and *Kommandant* Eberl.

Stangl was resolute in his desire to clear up the mess left by the former Commandant. A few days after he arrived, *SS-Oberscharführer* Kurt Franz, who had been appointed Stangl's deputy, arrived at the gates of Treblinka. Before the war Franz had joined the 3. Waffen-*SS-Totenkopfstandarte Thüringen*, and at the end of 1939 was summoned to the Führer's Chancellery and detailed for service as cook in the euthanasia institutes at Grafeneck, Hartheim, Sonnenstein and Brandenburg. As a member of the 6th Battalion he served at the Buchenwald concentration camp in 1941, and by the spring of 1942 had been ordered to the General Government, where he was posted to Belzec. He worked as a cook and trained the Ukrainian guards there before finally being given a new posting to Treblinka as Stangl's deputy. Franz described his arrival in Treblinka:

It was late summer or the beginning of autumn 1942 when I came from Belzec to Treblinka. I went by foot from the railway station of Malkinia to Treblinka; when I arrived it was already dark. Everywhere in the camp there were corpses. I remember that these corpses were already bloated. The corpses were dragged through the camp by working Jews ... These Jews were driven by the guardsmen [Ukrainians] and also by Germans ... I reported to Wirth in the dining room. As I remember, Wirth, Stangl, and Oberhauser were there.[22]

It did not take long before Franz made his mark at Treblinka, and soon became one of the most dominant SS men in the camp. The prisoners saw him as one of the cruellest and frightening figures and he was nicknamed *Lalke* (doll in Yiddish) owing to his baby face. Often he would be seen riding on his horse touring the camp, visiting the work sites in the Lower camp and the extermination area. When he was not roaming the camp he took part in the roll calls and the imposition of terrible punishments on the prisoners. He was accompanied by his new St Bernard Dog called Barry. Barry had been trained by Franz to be particularly ferocious, and upon his command he would attack Jews, biting at their bodies and sinking his sharp teeth in the victim's genitals, occasionally ripping them off.

A prisoner in the camp called Oscar Strawczinski wrote:

He walked through the camp with great pleasure and self confidence. Barry, his big, curly-haired dog, would lazily drag along behind ... 'Lalke' would never leave the place without leaving some memento for somebody. There was always some reason to be found. And even if there were no reason – it made no difference. He was an expert at whipping, 25 or 50 lashes. He did it with pleasure, without hurrying. He had his own technique for raising the whip and striking it down. To practise boxing, he would use the heads of Jews, and naturally there was no scarcity of those around. He would grab his victim's lapel and strike with the other hand. The victim would have to hold his head straight so that Franz could aim well. And indeed he did this expertly. The sight of the Jew's head after a 'training session' of this sort is not difficult to imagine. Once 'Lalke' was strolling along the platform with a double-barreled shotgun in his hand and Barry in his wake. He discovered a Jew in front of him, a neighbour of mine from Czestochowa by the name of Steiner. Without a second thought, he aimed the gun at the man's buttocks and fired. Steiner fell amidst cries of pain. 'Lalke' laughed. He approached him, commanded him to get up, pull down his pants, and then glanced at the wound. The Jew was beside himself with pain. His buttocks were oozing blood from the gashes caused by the lead bullets. But 'Lalke' was not satisfied. He waved his hand and said: 'Damn it, the balls haven't been harmed!' He continued to stroll to look for a new victim.[23]

The change of command in the camp notwithstanding, the brutality continued mercilessly. In early September Stangl moved into Eberl's quarters and Wirth, for nearly a month, was in a guest room next to him. The newly appointed *Kommandant* of Treblinka and the inspector of the death camps both immediately set about reorganizing the camp. As for Eberl, he returned to Bernberg euthanasia institution without being charged. According to his superiors he had deserved prosecution for not organizing the mass murder of men, women, and children in a more effective manner. To someone like Wirth, who had adapted the killing technique and ordered the smooth functioning of the 'Reinhard' camps, Eberl had totally misunderstood the concept of a death factory like Treblinka. In the eyes of Wirth he had not organized the system well enough, but his only saving grace was that he had achieved an exceptional killing rate.

SS-Reichsführer Heinrich Himmler at the airport in Paderborn, Germany. Himmler was the architect of genocide and was the Nazi leader most associated with the conception and operation of the liquidation of the Jewish race. USHMM (United States Holocaust Memorial Museum)

Out on the Eastern Front and SS *Polizei* forces prepare to undertake actions. When the Germans unleashed their attack against the Soviet Union on 22 June 1941, the Jewish problem escalated. For the Nazi empire the prospect of a war against Russia entailed a transition from one policy of murder to another, far more ambitious. In the eyes of Hitler the Soviet Union represented the home of Bolshevism and international Jewry, which he said needed to be rooted out and destroyed. HITM ARCHIVE (History in the Making)

SS *Polizei* forces in a wooded area. Virtually all the SS accepted their orders automatically, and soon became accustomed to the daily butchery. Some were actually addicted to the killings, whilst the majority accepted it as an order and a duty, and 'just got on with it'. HITM ARCHIVE

Above: Barry, the St Bernard dog, sitting for a photograph, probably taken by *SS-Oberscharführer* Kurt Franz. Barry had been trained by Franz to be particularly ferocious, and upon his command he would attack Jews. H.E.A.R.T. (Holocaust Education and Archive Research Team)

Left: Barry as a pup. Often Franz would be seen roaming Treblinka with Barry, sometimes strolling along the platform with a double-barrelled shotgun in his hand and Barry following behind. H.E.A.R.T.

Because of the huge flood of transports more prisoners were required to be selected for work detail to bury the thousands of people that were gassed and shot. *Kommandant* Eberl ordered that more burial pits were to be dug, and this was only partially completed by an excavator, seen here moving sand and earth in the pits. Top left: ARC (www.deathcamps.org) The excavator had been brought over from Treblinka I and was used every day to help bury the dead and dig corpse pits. The excavator was built by Menck & Hambrock, a type 'Ma', produced between 1933 and 1944. Power: 70 H.P., weight: 27 tons. These photos were taken by Stangl's deputy Kurt Franz. The photos left and above were found in his Treblinka album *Schöne Zeiten* (Pleasant Times). ARC

SS-men on the buckets of the excavator. These photographs were probably taken in the first half of 1943. At least two types of excavators were used in Treblinka, bucket and cable excavators. It was later realized that the bucket excavator was not very effective for digging burial pits. ARC

Deportation of Jews from the General Government either in the late winter of 1942, or early 1943. HITM

A Jewish man waits with women and children prior to boarding a train for an unknown destination in the East. These people had been told that they were being resettled further East and that it was important to take all their luggage and belongings with them. HITM

Jewish men, women and children with their belongings preparing to board a train to an unknown destination. During mid-1942 a whole series of resettlement 'actions' were being conducted right across occupied Poland. These actions saw the vast majority of Jews being sent directly to Belzec, Sobibor and Treblinka. Ninety-five per cent of all arrivals at these camps were dead within three hours. HITM

Clockwise from above: Two photographs showing two SS officers belonging to an unidentified police unit in the East during the winter of 1942. Throughout 1942 and the following year the SS police and special action killing squads undertook various operations combing the countryside for Jews and partisans and any other people they regarded as hostile to their regime. HITM

A photograph taken probably during the late summer of 1942 showing Stangl and his deputy Franz at a doorway to the SS barracks. Stangl is wearing his familiar white tunic and holding an ox-hide whip. ARC

Dr Eberl. Eberl was the first commandant of Treblinka, and he ruled the camp with an iron fist. As soon as he took command he was determined to deliver an exceptional killing rate that far outstripped that of any other camp in the Nazi empire. H.E.A.R.T.

A portrait of Hermann Felfe. He oversaw the construction of the first water tower in Camp I. H.E.A.R.T.

A portrait of Alfred Forker. He was posted to Treblinka in 1942 and undertook guard duties in Camp II. His duties also included the sorting yard. H.E.A.R.T.

SS-Unterscharführer Fritz Schmidt alighting from a vehicle in the grounds of Treblinka. Schmidt operated the gas chamber engines in the camp. H.E.A.R.T.

SS-Oberscharführer Willy Matzig. He was book-keeper/accountant and was one of Stangl's two senior administrative assistants. His office was in Stangl's quarters. He was also part of the squad that received prisoners on the platform when deportations arrived. H.E.A.R.T.

SS-Sturmbannführer Christian Wirth (middle) accompanied by other SS officers during a tour of one of the *Reinhard* camps. Wirth soon earned himself a reputation and was nicknamed 'savage Christian'. Wirth realized that by killing large numbers of people in one location he had broken completely away from the conventional purpose of a concentration camp. H.E.A.R.T.

Clockwise from above: SS-Rottwachmeister Willy Grossmann. His main duties were in Camp II and he also received prisoners on the platform when deportations arrived. H.E.A.R.T.

The small station building of the Treblinka village. Here all deportation transports were broken up and shunted to the camp. The station master Zabecki received all transport telexes and stored them here. The brick building was built by the Germans, it replaced the old wooden one. ARC

This photo was taken in August 1942 when Pötzinger visited the Treblinka cook August Hengst and his wife Augusta in Warsaw. During an interrogation after the war Hengst told about this visit. He was allowed to wear civilian clothes, and he had an apartment in Warsaw where he often welcomed visitors from Treblinka. At this time Hengst was busy getting food and other goods for the Treblinka camp staff. From time to time he had to travel to Treblinka. When Pötzinger and Pinnemann made this visit, they decided to go to a photographic studio in the same road, where this photo was taken. ARC

Ukrainian troops during the Warsaw uprising observe a number of dead Jews at the entrance to a bombed-out building. During the third week of April 1943 a few hundred Jews in Warsaw had organized an armed uprising. Fighting was so

intense that the Germans had been compelled to send in over 2,000 well-armed troops. The majority of Jews that survived the uprising were sent directly to Treblinka. M. Kaludow/Bundesarchiv

Jewish men and women rounded up by a German police unit in Warsaw during the uprising. Approximately 13,000 Jews were killed in the ghetto during the uprising.

Of the remaining 50,000 residents, most were rounded up destined for Treblinka.
M. Kaludow/Bundesarchiv

The camp zoo constructed near the Ukrainian barracks on the orders of Stangl in the early summer of 1943. Here the SS spent their leisure time sitting on wooden benches and tables relaxing and looking at the animals. ARC

From left to right, *SS-Unterscharführer* Paul Bredow (Head of 'Barracks A', which was the clothing sorting barracks); *SS-Unterscharführer* Willi Mentz, who was assigned to Camp II in the summer of 1942 and then to Camp I as chief *Landwirtschaftskommando* (Agricultural Command); *SS-Unterscharführer* Max Moller (posted to Camp I as ordinance, 'Undressing Yard', and farming); and *SS-Scharführer* Josef Hirtreiter, nicknamed 'Sepp' by his comrades (posted to Treblinka in October 1942 until October 1943. His main duties were in Camp II). H.E.A.R.T.

This ammunition storeroom was located between the two SS barracks. It was built during the first phase of the camp as a concrete cube. In spring 1943 a second storey was added, containing a water tank to supply new showers for the SS staff. During the revolt the SS barracks burned down. This photo was taken by Kurt Franz, after the revolt. (A number of these photos are from the Kurt Franz Album he called *Schöne Zeiten,* 'Pleasant Times'.) ARC

An aerial view taken during an Allied reconnaissance mission over Poland in 1944, showing the former site of the Treblinka death camp. ARC

Above: Looking for the truth – or for profit – after the camp had been dismantled.

Left: Franz Stangl.

Memorial stones at Treblinka today. Adjacent to the huge tombstone (the crack
is part of the design) is a symbolic graveyard containing 17,000 'gravestones'

representing the towns and villages from which the dead were transported. The stone representing Warsaw is the biggest.

SS-Untersturmführer
Dr.med.Irmfried Eberl
warschau

Was als Brühl/SS- und Polizeiführer   Warschau, den 19.6.1942

Der Kommissar
für den jüdischen Wohnbezirk
in Warschau

An den

Kommissar für den jüdischen Wohnbezirk

_W A R S C H A U_

Für das Lager Treblinka werden noch benötigt:

10 m 1/4 Zoll Kupferrohr
5-10 kg Schweissdrahtstangen
2 kg Messingdraht zum Hartlöten
Je 50 m Eisenrohr: 1 Zoll, 3/4 Zoll, 1/2 Zoll
Je 20 Eisenrohr-T-stücke: 1 Zoll, 3/4 Zoll, 1/2 Zoll
Je 30 Stück Eisenrohr-Kniestücke: 1 Zoll, 3/4 Zoll, 1/2 Zoll
Je 20 Stück Dos einnipel (Verbindungsstücke): 1 Zoll, 3/4 Zoll, 1/2 Zoll
6 wasserdichte Lichtarmaturen mit Fassung, verschliessbar mit Gitter
10 Wasserhähne 3/4 Zoll mit Schlauchanschluss
10 Wasserhähne 1/2 Zoll mit Schlauchanschluss
Elektrische Glühbirnen 120 Volt: 30 Stück 25 Watt
                                  20 Stück 60 Watt
                                  20 Stück 75 Watt
                                  20 Stück 100 Watt

500 m 2 adrige G.A. Litze
1000 m Freileitungsdraht 2,5 ø
Freileitungsglocken

H e i l H i t l e r !

[signature]

---

eneraldirektion der Ostbahn
33H Bfp 16 Bfsv   Krakau, den 15. Sept. 1942

Fahrplananordnung Nr 587
Nur für den Dienstgebrauch!

An
Bfe, Baui der Strecken Sedziszow - Kielce - Skarzysko Kam. - Radom -
Deblin - Lukow - Siedlce - Malkinia; Kielce - Tschenstochau; Bf Treb-
linka; Bf Kozienice;
Bw Sedziszow, Kielce, Tschenstochau, Skarzysko Kam., Radom, Deblin,
Lukow, Siedlce, Malkinia;
Zl Tschenstochau, Siedlce; ZÜ Radom;
OHD, Ozl, Bzp Warschau, Radom;
Gedob: BÜ, BÜ(Lok, B 41, Bfp 3, 14, 15, 16, 17, 22, 44; L 2, 3, 71,
       Vt 11, VK I (5), Wg 1,
       Ref 7, 9, 21, 21H, 30, 31, 32, 33, 34, 34H, 36, 37;

Es verkehren folgende Sonderzüge für Umsiedler aus dem Bezirk Radom:

1.) Leerzug Lp Kr 9220 nach Fahrplananordnung Nr 582 ist von Treb-
    linka nicht nach Tschenstochau, sondern nach Sedziszow zu leiten:
    Kielce an   6.41   am 20.9, ab 6.51 im Plan Dg 91266 B,
    Sedziszow an 9.20

    In Sedziszow ist der Wagenzug bis 21.9. abzustellen.

2.) P Kr 9228 (30.9) Sedziszow - Treblinka am 21./22. Sept.

    Sedziszow   16.16 im Plan Dg 91253 B
    Kielce   18.56/19.55   "   " Dg 91255 B
    Skarzysko Kam. 21.41/22.43 "   " Dg 91255 B
    Radom   0.03/ 0.28   "   " Dg 91557 B
    Deblin Gbf   2.30/ 3.10   "   " Dg 91257 B
    Lukow   5.17/ 6.08   "   " Dg 95402 B
    Siedlce   6.58/ 8.34   "   " Dg 91365 B
    Treblinka   11.24/(15.59)

    Wagenzug: 2 C + 50 G.

3.) Rückleitung des Leerzuges:

    Lp Kr 9229 (30.11) von Treblinka nach Szydlowiec am 22./23.Sept.

    Treblinka   (11.24)/15.59 im Plan Dg 91368 B
    Siedlce   17.56/18.42   "   " Dg 9144' B
    Radom   19.36/30.37   "   " Dg 91266 B
    Deblin Gbf   22.34/23.36   "   " Dg 91266 B
    Radom   1.34/ 1.50   "   " Dg 91266 B
    Szydlowiec   3.08/21.30)

3.) Lp Kr 9230 (30.9) von Szydlowiec nach Treblinka am 23./24. Sept.

    Szydlowiec   (5.05)/21.30   im Plan Dg 91249 B
    Radom   22.29/ 0.13   "   " Dg 91555 B
    Deblin Gbf   2.00/ 3.10   "   " Dg 91257 B
    Lukow   5.17/ 6.08   "   " Dg 95402 B
    Siedlce   6.58/ 8.34   "   " Dg 91365 B
    Treblinka   11.24/(15.59)

00053

Mit Maschinenschrift auszufüllen!

Bewerbung um Verwendung in der Sicherheits-
==
polizei und im SD für die Kolonien.
==

Name: **S t a n g l**

Vorname: **Franz**

Geboren am: **26. März 1908**

    in: **Altmünster**

SS-Dienstrang: **Oberscharführer**

Pol.-Dienststellung: **Kriminaloberassistent**

Dienststelle: **Geheime Staatspolizei**

Bei Abordnung auch Heimatdienststelle:

Wohnung (Ort,Straße): **Wels, Leopold Bauerstrasse 7**

Familienstand (led. verh. gesch. verw.): **verheiratet**

Kinder (Zahl,Alter): **zwei Mädchen im Alter von 3 und 4 Jahren**

Schulbildung (Abschlußprüfung): **Volks- und 3 Kl.Bürgerschule(Haupt)**

Berufsausbildung (vor Eintritt in Polizei oder SD): **Textilbetriebsmeister (Weberei und Webereivorbereitung)**

Polizeiliche Prüfungen (auch Sonderausbildung): **2 Jahre Schutzpolizei-ausbildung mit Abschlussprüfung, Kriminalbeamtenkurs mit Abschluss-prüfung.**

Sprachkenntnisse (geläufig od.schulmäßig): **engl. und latein schulmäßig**

Technische Kenntnisse (Führerscheine,Zeichnen,funktechn.Kenntn.): **Führerschein ,Klasse 1,3 und 4; Staatsgewerbeschule für Autobau mit Abschlussprüfung;**

Treblinka documents. Above left: Orders for copper pipes, iron and other building materials needed for Treblinka signed by Irmfried Eberl. Above: Train timetables for Treblinka. *Nur für den Dienstgebrauch!* – for official use only. *Ruckleitung des Leerzuges* refers to the return of the empty wagons. Left: Franz Stangl's application, giving his schooling and previous work record and showing he was married with two children, girls aged three and four. He had a little schoolboy-level English and Latin. H.E.A.R.T.

Chapter III

Under the Command of Franz Stangl *(phase two)*

As soon as Wirth arrived in Treblinka to reorganize the camp after sacking Eberl he ordered the SS personnel to murder all the prisoners who had worked in the extermination area removing and burying the bodies. Wirth made it clear to the officers that secrecy in the camp was paramount and contact between the Jews employed in the extermination area and those in the Lower Camp was prohibited. Suspension of the transports was also instigated, in order for work to commence on clearing up the corpses near the ramp and around the reception area. Once again, to retain utmost secrecy, Wirth ordered that the Jews who had remained from the last transports carry out the gruesome task and were left alive at Stangl's discretion until the work was completed. Wirth guided the staff and spoke at length about how to handle the transports properly in an organized and efficient manner. *SS Scharführer* Suchomel:

> I remember that in the time when the whole camp was entirely disorganized, Wirth conducted talks with the German staff, mainly at 11 o'clock in the evening. These talks took place in the presence of the transports and with the incorporation of the Jewish working commando in this process. His instructions were detailed. For example, these described how to open the doors of the freight cars, the disembarking of the Jews, and the passage through the 'tube' to the upper part of the camp. Wirth personally gave an order that when the Jews were taking off their

shoes they had to tie them together … Wirth's instructions were carried out even after he left Treblinka.[24]

Wirth was fully aware that the reorganization of Treblinka would have to be undertaken quickly and effectively, and this was done with an iron fist. As Franz Suchomel testified,

> From my activity in the camps of Treblinka and Sobibor, I remember that Wirth in brutality, meanness, and ruthlessness could not be surpassed. We therefore called him 'Christian the Terrible' or 'The Wild Christian'. The Ukrainian guardsmen called him 'Stuka'. The brutality of Wirth was so great that I personally see it as a perversity. I remember particularly that on each occasion, Wirth lashed Ukrainian guardsmen with a whip he always kept …[25]

By the second week of September, Globocnik made it known that the liquidation of the Warsaw ghetto could not be postponed much longer. Eichmann had been kept well informed of the situation and would undoubtedly be pressing for transports to commence very shortly.

One of the most important tasks that both Wirth and Stangl needed to undertake for restructuring the killing operation was the reception of new arrivals. During Eberl's time at the camp there had been insufficient manpower to deal with them, so Wirth ordered that an adequate number of Jewish workers be given the job of waiting at the train platform. They were charged with removing the bodies of those that had died en route and taking them to the pits. They were also to escort those incapable of walking from the trains to the gas chambers. Wirth ordered that an additional pit be prepared in the southern corner of the camp, near the train platform.

Perhaps the most important reorganization of the camp that Wirth instigated was the construction of the new gas chambers, which began in early September. This was one of Stangl's first priorities as *Kommandant,* to erect a new building for the gas chambers beside the old one. Construction of the building was carried out whilst the old gas chambers were still being operated. Wirth dispatched SS-*Scharführer* Lorenz Hackenholt, who was in charge of the gas chambers at Belzec, to assist in the construction of the new ones in Treblinka.

The new building comprised six gas chambers, each 4 x 8 metres in size. The combined area they covered was 192 square metres. The designers ensured that these new structures would be more efficient. The height of the new gas chambers was slightly lower than the older ones. By lowering the height of the chambers, the cubic volume was reduced, thus reducing the total gas needed for murdering the victims and shortening the asphyxiation time. In the old chambers there had been instances where very young children had not suffocated properly because the gas had not filled the entire space. Now with lower ceilings the designers were confident that the chambers would be more efficient and save time processing the victims.

Those entering the building found it decorated with plants, and the entrance to the corridor covered by a thick dark Jewish ceremonial curtain pillaged from a synagogue. On it was inscribed in Hebrew: 'This is the Gateway to God. Righteous men will pass through.' Over the entrance to the door was a large Star of David. To access the door, one climbed five wide steps with potted plants on either side.

The six new gas chambers were capable of murdering 2,300 people simultaneously, whereas the old ones could only hold 680. So that the killing process could be observed, there was a specially designed peephole fitted in the door consisting of a double pane of glass.

The first transport to Treblinka under Stangl's command arrived from Warsaw on 4 September 1942. Wirth and Stangl were on the platform when the train shunted into the station. The newly appointed *Kommandant* watched the Jews get processed from the platform to the 'tube'.

SS-Oberscharführer Heinrich Matthes, who was in charge of Camp II, described the killing operations there:

> During the entire time that I was in Treblinka, I served in the Upper Camp ... About fourteen Germans carried out services in the Upper Camp. There were two Ukrainians permanently in the Upper Camp. One of them was called Nikolai, the other was a short man, I don't remember his name ... These two Ukrainians who lived in the Upper Camp served in the gas chambers. They also took care of the engine room when Fritz Schmidt was absent. Usually this Schmidt was in charge of the engine room. In my opinion, as a civilian he was either a mechanic or driver. He came from Pirna ... The people who were brought through the passage were forced to enter the separate gas chambers. Later, in the

summer of 1942, the new gas chambers were built. I think that they became operational only in the autumn. Altogether, six gas chambers were active. According to my estimate, about 300 people could enter each gas chamber. The people went into the gas chambers without resistance. Those who were at the end, the Ukrainian guards had to push inside. I personally saw how the Ukrainians pushed people with their rifle butts … The gas chambers were closed for about 30 minutes. Then Schmidt stopped the gassing, and the two Ukrainians who were in the engine room opened the gas chambers from the other side.[26]

The Ukrainian guards had been assigned by the SS to undertake wide-ranging guard duties and assisted the SS with new arrivals, ensuring that no one attempted to escape, and oversaw the undressing and escort to the gas chambers. One of their main tasks was to supervise the gas chambers and work the motor that supplied the gas to the gas chamber. It was here that the Ukrainians had daily contact with the prisoners who worked in the extermination area, which gave them the opportunity to inflict unrestrained brutality on their victims. Eli Rozenberg who was a prisoner working in the extermination area wrote about one particular Ukrainian's behaviour. His name was Ivan Demaniuk and he was nicknamed 'Ivan the Terrible'.

This Ukrainian took special pleasure in harming other people, especially women. He stabbed the women's naked thighs and genitals with a sword before they entered the gas chambers and also raped young women and girls. The ears and noses of old Jews which weren't to his liking he used to cut off. When someone's work wasn't to his satisfaction, he used to beat the poor man with a metal pipe and break his skull. Or he would stab him with his knife. He especially enjoyed entwining people's head between two strands of barbed wire and then beating the head while it was caught between the wires. As the prisoner squirmed and jumped from the blows, he became strangled between the wires.[27]

Whilst the new gas chambers were being constructed Stangl was determined that the camp would not descend into the previous chaos. He knew his job there depended on running the camp efficiently, and required his personnel to maintain a degree of restraint in front of the new arrivals. However, when Stangl arrived, the SS and their Ukrainian counterparts continued routinely to murder men, women and children as they saw fit. They had become hardened to the cruelties they practised and indifferent to the sufferings they inflicted. Eberl had developed a close personal contact and rapport with his men unusual even in the SS, inspiring a near worshipful devotion from SS soldiers who both feared and revered him. Stangl was determined to re-form the camp and the SS that served there. To his SS officers he preached the need for rooting out from the ranks the disobedient, the unreliable, and the lazy. The frequent announcements of such dismissals, transfers, and punishments in the weekly circulars of Stangl's inspectorate demonstrate the disciplinary thoroughness he exacted. Yet these men he commanded were not automatons – they were individual men, with individual personalities. Some were worse, some were better. What they all had in common was limitless power over their victims.

Most of the SS men serving in the camp were inspired and comforted by the thought of home, believing that when they got leave they could recapture the life they once possessed before being posted to the camp. But it was not possible. Treblinka altered everyone that worked there. Though they never sought to change their comfortable existence in the camp, a few were quite aware of the psychological burden they had to carry.

On leave the SS men either went back to the Homeland or remained in Poland where there families had taken up residence in the nearby cities of Warsaw or Lublin. Here they all enjoyed a life style infinitely more agreeable than anything they could enjoy whilst fighting on the frontline. It soon became a close-knit community where SS wives would visit each other, gossip, hold afternoon tea parties, and invite husbands along for evening drinks and dinner. As for the children, they would either attend private schools in the city, or be taught by a privately hired governess. When the children were not attending school, they were looked after by domestic slaves that cooked meals and cleaned their nicely furnished homes.

Behind this façade the SS men were hiding the terrible truth about their posting, and most avoided ever uttering a single word about the killings. As far as they were concerned their family members were not aware of the barbaric measures taken against the Jews in the concentration camps. And yet, as a whole, these were not naïve people. They probably knew, but subconsciously chose not to associate their loved one with the murders. In their eyes he was a dear son or a loving husband, not capable of brutality in any measure, even against the Jews, their sworn enemy.

Some of the SS men did develop an intense desire to tell the truth, especially to those close to them. Some wanted to broadcast boastfully to the world about what a great job they were doing. But the majority felt bound by honour and duty to the SS order to carry out their gruesome crimes in secret. The psychological impact on some of them was sometimes severe. *SS-Unterscharführer* Kurt Arndt, who worked in Camp II, one day broke silence about Treblinka and spoke about the death camp in a bar. He was later charged, removed from the camp and sent to Sachsenhausen concentration camp.

The change of command at Treblinka did not reduce the terrible atrocities being committed there, but allowed the process of murder to function more effectively. Thanks to Stangl and Wirth's initiatives, after the construction of the new gas chambers the reduction in the delays to the train journey to the camp had significantly reduced the need for the corpse pits for those dead on arrival. This meant that those that lacked sufficient strength to walk on their own to the gas chambers could now be executed at these pits. The area set aside for the execution by shooting could also be reduced in size, and it was agreed by Wirth that the area be given the appearance of a hospital, which became known in the camp as *Lazarett*. This area measured 150 to 200 square metres and was surrounded by barbed-wire and foliage. The entrance to the *Lazarette* area had a large Red Cross sign erected to dupe the deportees.

SS-Scharführer August Miete was put in charge of the *Lazarett*. He was soon nicknamed the 'Angel of Death' by the prisoners. He described the *Lazarett*:

> There were always sick and crippled people in the transports … There were also those who had been shot and wounded en route by the SS, policemen, or Latvians who guarded the transports. These ill, crippled, and wounded passengers were brought to the *Lazarett* by a special group of workers. Inside the *Lazarett* they placed or lay these people at the edge of the pit. When all the sick and wounded had been brought, it was my job to shoot them. I fired at the nape of the neck with a 9mm pistol. Those shot would fall … into the pit … The number of people shot in this way from each transport varied. Sometimes two or three, and sometimes twenty or even more. They included men and women, and old, and also children.[28]

SS-Unterscharführer Willi Mentz, known as the 'Gunman' of Treblinka, worked inside the *Lazarett* and became a much-feared figure among the Jewish work-brigades. Wearing a white doctor's smock he was to shoot thousands of helpless Jews, pushing their blood-soaked bodies into the pit. To the prisoners of Treblinka, Mentz became known as 'Frankenstein'. Mentz wrote:

> I was transferred to the so-called hospital area. This so-called hospital was in the lower camp in a special zone which was fenced off and protected against onlookers by pine branches. In this area there was a large mass grave. This grave was dug by an excavator and must have been about seven metres deep.
>
> Next to the mass grave there was a small wooden hut which was used by the two members of the Jewish working commando who were on duty in the 'hospital'. These Jews wore armbands marked with a red cross. That was Kuttner's idea – he was responsible for the lower camp.
>
> Following the arrival of a transport, six to eight cars would be shunted into the camp, coming to a halt at the platform there. The commandant, his deputy Franz, Kuttner and Stadie or Matzig would be there waiting as the transport came in. Further SS members were also present to supervise the unloading: for example, Genz and Belitz had to make absolutely sure that there was no one left in the car after the occupants had been ordered to get out.
>
> When the Jews had got off, Stadie or Matzig would have a short word with them. They were told something to the effect that they were a resettlement transport and that they would be given a bath and that they would receive new clothes. They were also instructed to maintain quiet and disciplined. They would continue their journey the following day.
>
> Then the transports were taken off to the so-called 'transfer' area. The women had to undress in huts and the men out in the open. The women were then led through a passageway, known as the 'tube', to the gas-chambers. On their way they had to pass a hut where they had to hand in their jewelry and valuables. The shed was manned by two work-Jews and a member of the SS. The SS member was Suchomel.
>
> After they had undressed the men had to put their and the women's clothes in an orderly pile in a designated place. That only happened in the early days of after the reorganization. Later on there were special working

commandos, which would immediately sort the clothes the transport participants had taken off.

There were always some ill and frail people on the transports. Sometimes there were also wounded people amongst the arrivals because the transport escorts, SS members, police, Latvians, sometimes shot people during the journey. These ill, frail and wounded people would be taken to the hospital by a special working commando. These people would be taken to the hospital area and stood or laid down at the edge of the grave. When no more ill or wounded were expected it was my job to shoot these people. I did this by shooting them in the neck with a 9-mm pistol. They then collapsed or fell to one side and were carried down into the grave by the two hospital work Jews. The bodies were sprinkled with chlorinated lime. Later, Wirth's instructions, they were burnt in the grave itself.

The number of people I shot after the transport arrived varied. Sometimes it was two or three but sometimes as many as twenty or perhaps even more. There were men and women of all ages and there were also children.[29]

The words of Metz echo almost exactly those of Miete. The *Lazarett* was deemed by Stangl as the only effective means of processing Jews deemed too sick or weak to walk to the gas chambers. He was not so much interested in the numbers murdered, as the former *Kommandant* had been, but more eager to run the camp efficiently and with the least psychological impact on those that worked there and those deportees waiting to be processed, the latter in order to retain order. He already knew from previous experience that panic and fear among the new arrivals had a deleterious effect on their jailers and disrupted the work. Yet, this is exactly what happened on 11 September 1942. On this day a prisoner selection was carried out when a new transport arrived. The selection was carried out by *SS-Scharführer* Max Bielas and another SS man. All workers from the old detail were stood in a line whilst Bielas handpicked the men he deemed weak, and who were to be killed. One of the workers, named Berliner, suspected the worst and suddenly left the line and attacked Bielas pushing a blade into his back. As the fatally wounded SS man fell to the floor in a pool of blood other SS personnel and Ukrainian guards came running over to assist their wounded comrade. What followed was panic and confusion:

SS-men came … They looked petrified … Berliner did not even try to escape. He stood quite composed, with a strange, mild smile in his face … But a few minutes later was lying on the ground with his face smashed. Blood flowed from his mouth … Bielas died of his wounds a few days later … Two other Jews were killed with spades. The Ukrainians started beating people around frantically … The commandant ordered 'Lalka' to shoot ten Jews.[30]

Over the next few weeks very few men were selected from the transports, the majority were simply unloaded and sent straight to be processed. More and more shipments arrived. Between October until the end of December Treblinka reached its peak. Sometimes there were as many as six trainloads – 20,000 people a day. Initially these mostly comprised Jews from Warsaw, then many started to arrive from Germany and other parts of Western Europe. They brought with them enormous quantities of food, money and jewels. There was a huge assortment of liquor taken from new arrivals. When off duty in the barracks both the SS and the Ukrainians enjoyed all the varieties that were distributed among them. Generally, the SS did not feel any different towards a Jewish group from one particular country ot another, unless they were keen on a particular beverage such as vodka or schnapps. Often they would go to bed drunk or would simply collapse where they sat drinking.

The personnel at Treblinka, it appears, had thus manufactured for themselves what they considered to be a tolerable life. Their posting was relatively easy, and they had as much food to eat and alcohol to drink as they wanted. To the SS, the camp was very much like a small town. It had a vegetable shop where you could also buy bones to make broth. There was a canteen, a cinema, a theatre with regular performances and a sports club. Generally the personnel worked well together, in spite of some rivalry.

Outside Treblinka the local Poles lived off the proceeds of the camp. All the peasants came to barter, especially the farmers that tended their fields adjoining the perimeter of the camp. The Warsaw prostitutes too did plenty of business with the Ukrainian guards, and were regularly seen travelling by train to the camp. A number of Polish females from Warsaw and surrounding areas were also brought into the camp and they were employed in the kitchen and the laundry, in both the lower and upper camps. All the girls were handpicked and were young and attractive and there were relationships between the Ukrainians and some of the girls.

Stangl tolerated relationships with the females as long as it did not hinder the guards' work whilst on duty. He believed it made life more normal and tolerable. Other SS personnel, like Kuttner, however, despised the women in the camp and one day he sent a girl who was in a relationship with a man called Kuba to work in the laundry. They never saw each other again.

Kuttner was a nasty, low-natured individual, different from his superior Stangl. It did not take long before he began beating and killing the inmates. He was in charge of the Lower Camp. He would often follow people around, stop them and search them for hidden valuables. If he caught someone carrying anything, he would whip and beat them and have them sent to the *Lazarett*. He exploited every area of the camp he ruled, and turned some of the prisoners into informers.

One day when a transport arrived Kuttner removed ten or twelve young boys and gave them various duties around the camp. One of the boys was appointed Kapo of the group. After a few weeks, the boy was caught bribing one of the Ukrainian guards with gold coins, and Kuttner had him, along with all the other boys in the group, sent to the gas chambers.

At Christmas Stangl ordered the construction of a fake railway station. Originally the train platform where the deportees arrived was literally a ramp. But now, he wanted to enhance the illusion in order to fool the new arrivals into believing they had arrived at a genuine station to a transit camp. This was undertaken especially for those arriving from outside Poland, mainly from the West. A clock was painted with numerals and hands which never moved, a ticket-window was constructed, various timetables and arrows indicating train connections to Warsaw, Wolwonoce and Bialystock were plastered on the walls of the sorting barracks. There were fake doors and windows installed, a Waiting Room, Information Telegraph Office, Station Manager, and Rest Rooms. There were many trees and beds of flowers were planted.

To enhance the illusion he had the amateur musicians removed and replaced by professionals that were organized into a small orchestra. The famous Jewish conductor Artur Gold who had arrived in one of the transports and was already on his way to the 'tube' before being recognized, was ordered to organize the orchestra.

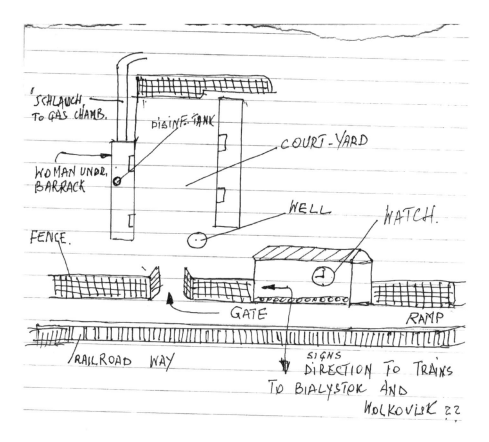

TEIGMAN SKETCH
Survivor Kalman Teigman drew this sketch of the 'station' and the undressing facilities.
(Courtesy of ARC)

Strange though it may seem a number of the higher ranking SS officers quite liked Gold, probably because he was known for the great lengths he went to to satisfy their needs. In fact, for his fortieth birthday a party was held in his honour in the tailor shop. Drinks and food were laid out and the orchestra performed in its gala clothes. For a couple of hours the orchestra played opera selections and operettas accompanied by singers and a choir. Stangl encouraged such behaviour. But he knew, as well as everyone else participating, it was a charade. Like so many that have endured terrible circumstances, escape from reality meant survival.

To make full use of Gold's musical talents Kurt Franz ordered him to compose a melody in German, which the prisoners were forced to memorise and sing during roll call, and whilst on work detail. The song was nicknamed 'The Anthem of Treblinka'.

> We look straight out at the world,
> The columns are marching off to their work.
> All we have left is Treblinka,
> It is our destiny.
>
> We heed the commandant's voice,
> Obeying his every nod and sign.
> We march along together
> To do what duty demands.
>
> Work, obedience, and duty
> Must be our whole existence.
> Until we, too, will catch a glimpse at last
> Of a modest bit of luck.

As if this was not enough Stangl allowed his deputy to order the orchestra to start playing at the evening roll call, whilst the selections of the sick took place, and occasionally when new shipments arrived. This was one of the most unusual ideas implemented at the camp, but Stangl was determined to lull the arriving transports in whatever way he had at his disposal. Initially, the fake station and the orchestra did not sit comfortably with his conscience – or so he claimed:

> It was months before I could look one of them in the eye. I repressed it all by trying to create a special place: gardens, new barracks, new kitchens, new everything; barbers, tailors, shoemakers, carpenters. There were hundreds of ways to take one's mind off it; I used them all … In the end, the only way to deal with it was to drink. I took a large glass of brandy to bed with me each night and I drank.[31]

It was easier for Stangl to look upon the upon the new arrivals as 'cargo'. He rarely saw them as individuals, rather as a huge mass of cargo waiting to be processed through his factory. Stangl often stood watching the new arrivals on the eastern wall between the two camps making sure that everything was running like clockwork. He tried to avoid seeing people in the undressing barracks, but watching them naked in their final minutes before going through the 'tube' was somehow easier, it made them no longer human to him. This was some kind of vile coping mechanism.

In order to repress his feelings, like some of the other SS men at Treblinka, he assumed a cold inhumanity. He did not get sentimental about the Jews and went about the camp in a businesslike manner, overseeing genocide like a director of a large corporation.

What also helped him during his posting to the camp was the thought of his wife and family. He was allowed on leave every three to four months. He had convinced himself, just as he had done in Sobibor, that home would allow him to recapture the life he once possessed before the war. However, his son Ludwig had told his mother about Sobibor, and their relationship had altered as a consequence. She had become very worried for him.

The first time Stangl came home on leave was for Chirstmas in 1942. Frau Stangl:

It was so wonderful to see him, and at Christmas too. In Austria, at home, what with Christmas and everything, what I knew was happening in Poland seemed utterly unreal. I asked about Treblinka of course, but he said he was only responsible for the valuables, construction and discipline. No, he didn't pretend then that it wasn't the same sort of place as Sobibor, but he said that he was doing everything he could to get out. He stayed home for eight or ten days, but he'd only been there a couple of days when he said he'd run over and see Fraulein Hintersteiner who had been a secretary at Hartheim and who afterwards worked for a man called Kaufmann who went out to the Crimea as police chief. Paul wanted her to help him get a transfer to the Crimea. When he came back from seeing her, he was very happy and said it was all right – all he had to do was wait to be notified of the transfer. So we had a good Christmas after all: I can still see his happy, relieved face.[32]

Stangl saw in the New Year, 1943, with his family in Austria. Whilst life continued more or less unchanged over the Christmas festivities many German families held their breath as news of bitter and bloody fighting on the Eastern Front arrived. On the radio, reports of heavy fighting at Stalingrad revealed that brave German legions of the sixth Army were still holding out in the besieged city and were inflicting maximum hardship and casualties on their hated Red foe. Yet it was clear by the first cold days of January that the war in Russia was not going to plan. Reverberations caused by the setback on the Eastern Front were increasingly felt at Treblinka. The rolling stock for transporting large shipments of Jews by rail was desperately needed by the army to move troops and other vital equipment from one part of the front to another as quickly as possible. Despite the inconvenience thousands of Jews were still being evacuated and successfully transported from all over Europe and the East and subjected to 'special treatment'. According to the chief statistician of the SS, Richard Korherr, who was responsible for compiling a progress report on the 'Final Solution', there had been approximately 2.7 million Jews exterminated in 1942 alone. The Operation Reinhard camps, notably Treblinka, Sobibor, Belzec, and a smaller camp called Majdanek, dominated the process of 'special treatment'.

German war production at the end of 1942 was suffering from a severe dearth of labour. The destruction of the Jewish ghettos in Poland had a serious impact on industrial production there. The deportation of the Jews to Treblinka from the Warsaw ghetto had, for instance, halved textile production. As more and more Jews were being murdered, the civilian and military authorities responsible for overseeing production in the occupied territories proposed that they at least retain those Jews who were engaged in war production. Senior SS officials in the General Government had also become deeply concerned. This was partly because the SS had employed considerable numbers of Jews in their lucrative businesses.

In early January 1943 the SS in the General Government began concentrating on all Jews that were fit or skilled workers and had been left behind during the evacuation of the ghettos. It was proposed that these Jews could be hired out to businesses for cash on a daily basis, returning to the labour camps at night.

The new proposal not to liquidate physically fit and skilled Jews had a significant effect on the 'Reinhard' camps. Although Jews would continue to be gassed in large quantities, the new policy meant that there would be fewer and fewer transports shipping their 'cargo' to the extermination centres of the General Government.

In the meantime, however, the 'Reinhard' camps were kept busy during early January because of problems with the completion of the new gas chambers at Auschwitz. Eichmann had been particularly eager to transfer

Jewish transports for immediate liquidation to Auschwitz, but was now reluctantly forced to redirect trains to Treblinka and Sobibor. Belzec had ceased its killing activity before the end of 1942. The redirection of the shipments to the two remaining 'Reinhard' camps was an administrative challenge, but thanks to Eichmann's experience and careful planning he was able to undertake the deliveries without too much difficulty.

Chapter IV

'Obermajdan' Treblinka
(phase three)

By mid-January 1943 there was a gradual decline in shipments to Treblinka. Whilst this seemed to offer a slight reprieve, conditions inside the camp for the living were appalling. The SS made no provisions for the sick, and those that fell ill or were unable to work were either shot or sent straight to the gas chambers. It was forbidden for the two Treblinka doctors – Dr Julian Chorazycki, who treated the German patients, and Dr Irka, who treated the Ukrainians – to treat sick Jews. The SS regularly followed the prisoners around the camp and scrutinized every one, making sure they did not show any signs of weakness or fatigue. At roll call those that appeared sick were dragged away to the *Lazarett* and murdered. When prisoners were too weak to walk to the *Lazarett* or gas chambers there were instances where they were killed by lethal injection. The injections were given by the prison doctors on orders of the SS. 'Death injections', as they became known, were also administered to prisoners that had gone mad.

The sanitary conditions had worsened terribly by the beginning of 1943. The living quarters of the prisoners were full of filth and rubbish and they could seldom change their ragged and unbelievably dirty clothing and linen. In the extermination area conditions for the prisoners were far worse as they slept in the same clothes for weeks at a time. Overcrowding in the living barracks was terrible, and disease rife. Throughout the camp the prisoners were infested with lice, which naturally, led frequently to the spread of spotted typhus. Because there was no procedure to combat typhus the mortality rate among able-bodied prisoners began to rise. There were

81

frequent typhus epidemics that killed hundreds. During these outbreaks the number of prisoners murdered by the SS increased dramatically.

The infirmary in the Lower Camp soon became full of sick and dying people. The SS would frequently wander around the infirmary, often with a handkerchief protecting their mouths, and order the Ukrainian guards to drag out the sick and have them shot in the *Lazarett*.

Inside the extermination area the conditions were far worse than anywhere else. There was no medical treatment, and every day dozens of people that fell sick were either shot or thrown into the gas chamber. So virulent was the infection that Stangl was deeply concerned that dysentery, typhoid fever, and typhus would spread from the inmates to his SS personnel and Ukrainian guards. Typhus was the most fatal of the three and therefore was the most feared among the Germans. The Germans had had experience of typhus during the First World War when they developed delousing units to control disease on the Eastern Front, where it was endemic. The soldiers were bathed and their clothes fumigated in mobile units, which killed the lice, but the lice were tenacious and were found in buildings, mattresses, and furniture.

In early February Stangl decided that the camp required urgent cleaning and disinfecting. For this purpose he brought an expert to the camp, along with disinfection equipment, from Majdanek. Kuttner organized a special disinfection group among the prisoners, which was then set to work spraying the buildings and barracks in the camp. In the extermination area Stangl ordered that a laundry be established, and a group of female prisoners from a new shipment be sent there to work. Lice still bred in many areas of the camp after the treatment and new hygiene regime. While the SS may have been only marginally successful in suppressing the disease, they were still extremely effective in suppressing the prisoners.

Many of the prisoners continued assisting the SS with unloading of the new arrivals and removing the dead from the gas chambers to the pits. Conditions were so terrible there were a number of attempted escapes. One day *SS-Scharführer* Josef Hirtreiter, nicknamed 'Sepp' by his comrades, brought two young boys to the centre of the roll call square who were caught trying to escape. Hirtreiter gave a short speech on the punishment of escapees and then ordered that the boys be hung naked by their feet. Another SS man with a whip proceeded to beat the boys for about an hour until they fell unconscious. Hirtreiter then killed them with a pistol.

Hirtreiter was a vicious individual who mainly worked in Camp II. He was born in Bruchsal and after extended elementary school he learned locksmithing but did not pass the final examination. Later he worked as a construction worker and bricklayer until he finally joined the Nazi Party in 1932. During the early part of the war he was ordered to the Hadamar euthanasia centre where he worked in the kitchen and the office. It was not until October 1942 that Hirtreiter was posted to Treblinka from Lublin. He came to the camp as a staunch Nazi and anti-Semite. As with many of the SS he perceived that the murder of the inferior peoples ensured Germany's long-term future in the East, and the German claim to dominance provided ideological justification for such acts of brutality.

Hirtreiter regularly hanged inmates for the slightest infringement of camp rules and left their contorted naked bodies for hours in the roll call square, as a warning to others. When he was not hanging, whipping, beating or shooting the prisoners he was assisting his fellow comrades unloading new arrivals. On a number of occasions he was seen pulling men, women and children out of the freight cars by their hair and seizing young children between the ages of one and two by their feet, and smashing their heads against the boxcars.

Off duty, Hirtreiter was regarded as a relatively quiet and thoughtful person. When on leave visiting his family, there was nothing that indicated that beneath the façade of the loving father, was a cold blooded torturer and mass murderer.

SS-Unterscharführer Paul Bredow was another man at Treblinka that showed no indication of his true self outside the camp. He had arrived in the camp with Stangl from Sobibor in late August 1942, and became head of 'Barracks A', which was the clothing sorting barracks. At Sobibor he had been in charge of the *Lazarett* where he practised target shooting on the Jews, shooting 50 of them a day. When he arrived at Treblinka it did not take long before he revealed his cruel nature. Once again, when off duty, in the company of his comrades in the barracks or mess, he never boasted of how he indiscriminately beat, whipped and killed Jews.

SS-Rottenführer Gustav Munzberger, was another man who never uttered a single word to his family and friends whilst on leave about how he sent thousands of Jews to their death each week in the gas chambers. He had arrived in Treblinka in late September 1942 and assisted *SS-Oberscharführer* Heinrich Matthes, operator of the gas chambers, and was in charge of the *Leichentransportkommando* (Body-Transport Team). Munzberger later recalled:

> When they sent me to Treblinka there was some administrative mix-up I think, and they gave me two different postings you know, two different pieces of paper. So I went to Wirth when I got to Treblinka and showed them to him and said could I please request permission to go to the other posting. But he sent me packing in no uncertain terms. He said the posting to Treblinka was more important than anything else – it overrode any other orders.[33]

According to Otto Horn, Munzberger was put in charge of the gas chambers, a task at which he excelled.

> One of his jobs was to stand at the door to the gas chambers and drive them in. He had a whip of course. He did that, day after day. He was drunk most of the time. What else could he do? Could he have got out of that job? I don't know. I think finally he no longer cared – he drank.[34]

Munzberger's son Horst recalls:

> At home, in the *Sudetenland*, my father was … well … a joiner, neither very good, nor bad – you know. But I can remember when he got that black SS uniform: that's when he began to be 'somebody' I suppose, rather than just anybody. And then, in Treblinka – it is inconceivable, isn't it, what he suddenly was: the scope, the power, the uniqueness, the difference between himself and all those others – imagine … No, it is unimaginable. I remember when I was a boy and he spanked me; he cried more than I did; he really did.[35]

Although Munzberger never revealed that he was in charge of the gas chambers at Treblinka, he did divulge something about the murderous activities going on in the camp while on leave one day to his inquisitive wife. Frau Munzberger was shocked by the revelation, but like so many other German citizens, she knew of the possible terrible retribution against her husband and family if she uttered the secret to anyone else.

Leaving his family for camp life was always difficult for Munzberger and although he approached his duties efficiently, inwardly he felt drained by the whole experience. Every day he was relieved when he came off duty. He later said: 'I could go down to my room and have peace … Our quarters were down in the lower camp.'[36] Here he would drink and try to chase away what he had witnessed earlier that day.

Other camp personnel were also drinking very heavily. They would regularly come off duty after a hard day's killing and carry on drinking. Light entertainment and pleasant music and jolly gatherings also provided many with further distraction and amusement. Some, like *SS-Unterscharführer* Kurt Meidkur, would often leave the camp and relax in the surrounding fields or forests. The days spent relaxing outside the camp alone or with his comrades, without any talk of camp duties, eased the burden. Outside the camp he felt insulated from the brutality, and when he walked through the forest crossing the main railway line that led directly to the camp he was able to avert from his eyes anything that displeased him. He for one felt because he did not work in the Upper Camp, he had nothing to do with the crude mechanics of the killing process, and therefore had tried to create for himself, like some of his comrades, a tolerable position in Treblinka by dissociating himself from the suffering and actual murder. But the sight of the beatings, the undressing of the new arrivals, the gassing installations and the burying of the corpses in the pits made this more or less impossible. They were all accomplices in murder, whether or not that had actually physically been involved in the killings. Many believed, or made themselves believe, that their victims were like pests or vermin that needed disposing of. In the main, the SS were not simply bloodthirsty, sadistic monsters. Their brutality was more learned than instinctive and emotional. The majority, if not all, nevertheless agreed with the process of murder at the camp.

By the end of January 1943, rumours had circulated that the war on the Eastern Front had deteriorated. Throughout the month the *Wehrmacht* had suffered unimaginable casualties and huge losses of equipment. Nearly six hundred miles of the front had stagnated, with some battles being fought out in conditions similar to those in the First World War. From the frozen Baltic, around the city of Leningrad, south to the Lake Ilmem, and across the vast tall pine forest of the Rzhev salient, and then down to Orel, German forces had hardly moved in twelve bitter months of fighting.

Further south at Stalingrad the once vaunted forces of *Feldmarschall* von Paulus' *6.Armee* had surrendered, and this sent further shock waves through Himmler's domain. The *Reichsführer* had known that during Germany's early victories he had little to fear in the implementation of continent-wide deportations of Jews. It was this military success that fed Himmler's lust for more Jewish blood. By 1943, the military difficulties did not diminish his endless desire for widespread deportations of Jews, but even a man like Himmler could not ignore the military setback on the Eastern Front.

By February the war situation and the fact that transports were being sent elsewhere in the *Reich*, notably to Auschwitz, where the camp was now increasing its daily output by constructing larger gas chambers and crematoria, saw Treblinka's daily death toll plummet. Because there were now insufficient numbers of shipments arriving daily in the camp, there was an acute shortage of food and spare clothing. Whilst many of the prisoners starved, the SS personnel were on strict rations. Even alcohol, upon which many had relied heavily to perform their duties, had been restricted. Vodka had been the most popular drink consumed by both SS personnel and their Ukrainian counterparts. With stocks fast depleting a number of off-duty Ukrainian guards left the confines of the camp and went out to the nearby villages and farmsteads to acquire drink and food, and whatever other pleasures they could whilst roaming the countryside.

Stangl was under no illusion that his killing factory was in its final period of operation. The complete annihilation of the Jews in the General Government had almost been achieved. With fewer and fewer numbers being processed it was only a matter of time before the Reinhard camps would be shut down. Himmler had taken particular interest in the Reinhard camps and was well aware that they had already played a decisive role in the Final Solution. At his SS headquarters in Berlin he discussed the future role of the two remaining death camps, Sobibor and Treblinka. Belzec had been shut down at the end of 1942, but the *Reichsführer* had authorized Globocnik to extend the killing operations in the other two camps so that the surrounding areas could be finally cleansed of all remaining 'Jewish stock'. This included the final liquidation of the Warsaw ghetto. For Himmler the systematic cleansing of the Warsaw ghetto indicated the final and most crucial stage of 'Operation Reinhard'. For this reason the *Reichsführer* decided he was going to visit both camps, Sobibor and Treblinka. This much-publicised visit was to inspect the camps and determine their fate and that of the personnel.

In early March 1943, the *Reichsführer* journeyed to Poland where he visited the 'Action Reinhard' headquarters. From there, with an entourage of about twenty people including Eichmann and Globocnik, he travelled from Lublin to Sobibor, and then on to Treblinka. Himmler's delegation finally arrived at the camp by car. Flanked by motorcycle combinations for protection the camp gates were opened, and the motorcade slowly drove into the compound. Once inside the camp *Kommandant* Stangl with his deputy Kurt Franz greeted the *Reichsführer* and the delegation and they proceeded to the assembly square where the camp prisoners had gathered to listen to speeches. The first to take to the podium was Eichmann, who said to them that the Germans were going to organize a new Jewish country and all the valuables taken away from Jews would be used for Jewish purposes. All the prisoners would be taken away and drafted into the *Wehrmacht* to form a disciplinary unit.

The next person to address the prisoners was Stangl, followed by two of his staff officers. They told the prisoners of the new camp regulations and the serious consequences if they were broken. It was also outlined that every prisoner would now have their own file in which all offences would be catalogued. After the speeches all prisoners were returned to their barracks, where barrack leaders were waiting for them to take down their names. The registered prisoners were then issued with coloured and numbered triangular badges which were sewn onto their clothes. The prisoners were divided into groups according to where they lived.

In the meantime, Stangl and his deputy showed Himmler and the others around the site. As they strolled past various gangs of inmates working strenuously, the commandant spoke to Himmler and the delegation about the general purpose of each building they inspected. The entourage went to the *Lazarett*, quickly bypassing the huts, and subsequently inspected the extermination area, where they stayed for half an hour.

Himmler told Stangl that the camp required improvements, and this started with changing the name of the 'Treblinka' station to the covert name of 'Obermajdan'. He was impressed with the efficiency of the camp, but once again reiterated the need for improved sanitary conditions if the camp was to remain open and work efficiently. The shaving of the hair of the prisoners was very important too, and this would be undertaken every 20 days.

The *Reichsführer* learnt that despite his orders, the corpses of the Jews had been buried and not cremated. In order to reduce further outbreaks of disease in the camp and to destroy all traces of the mass extermination, he commanded that the corpses be disinterred and burnt.

Himmler left Treblinka infused with confidence, and made it known to Globocnik that he was so impressed with the 'Operation Reinhard' staff that he wanted to promote 28 members of the SS and German police. Christian Wirth was promoted to the rank of *SS-Sturmbannführer* and his adjutant, *SS-Oberscharführer* Oberhauser to the officer rank of *SS-Untersturmführer*, Stangl was promoted to the rank of *SS-Hauptsturmführer*. Globocnik noted that 'Stangl is the best camp commander and had the most prominent part in the whole action.'[37] Stangl's deputy, Franz, who held the rank of *SS-Oberscharführer*, was promoted to *SS-Untersturmführer*.

With many of the leading figures in the 'Reinhard' operations promoted, their last duty was to destroy the evidence of the murders they had committed at Belzec, Sobibor and Treblinka. Stangl was told that he was to cremate the victims and erase all traces of the Jews in the camp. Completion of the cremation was to be accomplished as quickly as possible.

In order to fulfil the 'cremation order' Stangl ordered a new huge excavator to be brought to the camp where it would be used to exhume the corpses and burn them on a massive pyre. The task of exhuming the corpses was immense, for there were probably 800,000 victims buried in the pits, and burning them would take a number of weeks. A large tank of oil was delivered a few days after Himmler's visit and in mid-March an experiment was performed on burning the corpses. Jankiel Wiernik, who worked at Treblinka II, described the work undertaken at Himmler's behest:

> It turned out that women burnt more easily than men did. So they were burnt first as kindling ... Every day the number of burnt bodies was registered ... Male corpses did not burn. So the workers poured some petrol on the bodies and thus burnt them. When a plane was spotted in the sky, the work was stopped and the bodies were covered with fir trees so that nobody in the plane would notice ... When a pregnant women was burnt, a belly would burst and the child would get outside and burn in its mum's lap.[38]

Although the excavator did much of the job of exhuming the corpses, this also had to be undertaken by hand, which was horrific. Because of disease and the unbearable smell most used handkerchiefs and rags to cover their mouth and nose as they dug into the blood-filled soil. A huge fire was built with wood and oil and the corpses were simply thrown on to the enormous pyre of burning rags, flesh and bone. The gangs of workers could not burn the corpses efficiently enough.

Stangl held a meeting about the problem and contacted Wirth who called for expert advice from Auschwitz, *SS-Oberscharführer* Herbert Floss. Since July 1942, Auschwitz had been exhuming the dead from their corpse pits and burning them on a huge grilles at ground level. This had served as a makeshift crematorium whilst waiting for the proper ones to be delivered. Floss arrived in the second half of March and immediately set about improvising new burning facilities by ordering large rails that were delivered by train on specially adapted flatbed railcars. *SS-Oberscharführer* Matthes, the commander of the 'extermination area' later said:

> *SS-Oberscharführer* or *SS-Hauptscharführer* Floss ... was in charge of the arrangements for cremating the corpses. The cremation took place in such a way that railway lines and concrete blocks were placed together. The corpses were piled on these rails. Brushwood was put under the rails. The wood was doused with petrol. In that way not only the newly accumulated corpses were cremated, but also those taken out from the graves.[39]

In Treblinka II the camp excavator dug a large hole and workers set about laying concrete foundations. A grid was then erected of five or six rails each 25–30 metres long. The 'diggers' and another special team, called the 'burning group' or *Feuerkolonne* then laid the corpses out along the grate two metres high and a fire was started beneath the structure. In total some 3,000 corpses could be burned simultaneously. Yechiel Reichman from the 'burning group' wrote:

> The SS 'expert' on body burning ordered us to put women, particularly fat women, on the first layer on the grill, face down. The second layer could consist of whatever was brought – men, women, or children – and so on, layer on top of layer ... Then the 'expert' ordered us to lay dry branches under the grill and to light them. Within a few minutes the fire would take so it was difficult to approach the crematorium from as far as 50 metres away ... The work was extremely difficult. The stench was

awful. Liquid excretions from the corpses squirted all over the prisoner-workers. The SS man operating the excavator often dumped the corpses directly onto the prisoners working nearby, wounding them seriously.[40]

As the decomposing flesh burned, black smoke poured skyward. The excavator then proceeded to build a huge embankment from the sandy soil some five metres high. Once the bodies had been burnt, in order to remove the mountains of hot ash a special squad of 'diggers' and prisoners were selected to shovel it out. These were known as ash groups or *Aschkolonne*. After clearance of the grates, the remaining ashes were pulverised. This was normally done on a concrete plate where prisoners pulverised remains of bones with wooden pounders.

Stangl and his staff were convinced that the hideous process would destroy any trace of their heinous crimes. But the biggest problem was how quickly the burnings could be undertaken. In order to increase the number of burnings six cremation sites were constructed, which were capable of burning up to 12,000 corpses simultaneously every day. The sites were situated near the mass graves in order to save time in transferring the corpses. All new arrivals that were processed were emptied out of the gas chambers and transported directly to the cremating rails. However, the burning groups found that the fresh corpses did not burn as well, so they were sprayed with fuel first.

The body burning went on day and night, and dependent on the wind direction, smoke from the burnings often blanketed the Lower Camp. The smoke and smell of burning flesh carried for many miles. The SS personnel working inside the camp buildings often kept all windows and doors shut, and whilst venturing outside masked their mouths, trying to avoid breathing in the smoke. In the surrounding forest the thick air clung to the trees with a terrible smell, which left an awful taste in the mouth.

The burnings at the camp brought widespread despondency among the personnel. Their gloom was not because they felt any type of sympathy for those that they were burning, but simply because it had generated additional work. When they had sent their victims to the gas chambers, or killed them in the *Lazarret* they were under the impression that once they had been disposed of in the pits, this meant the end of the matter. Now, they were ordered to dig up their victims and repeat the process, but in more grisly circumstances than before. When new shipments arrived at the camp the SS could now send them to their deaths knowing that their victims after being killed would be sent directly to the 'roasters' to be burnt to ashes. Psychologically this made the killings easier to deal with. Their crimes would now be burnt to ashes instead of being buried.

At the end of March transports into Treblinka increased with shipments of new arrivals from Bulgaria. When the Bulgarians arrived in the camp the SS were overjoyed to see that they had brought with them a lot of food. This was instantly distributed among the SS personnel and the Ukrainian guards. What was left fed the prisoners.

Following the Bulgarian shipment came a transport from Salonika. This transport had been initially destined for Auschwitz, but due to processing problems there it was redirected to Treblinka instead. Thankfully for Stangl the Greek shipment had brought with them more food and lots of luggage containing a treasure trove of of clothing and equipment. More transports were destined to arrive, which Stangl knew would transform conditions in the camp.

During April came deportees from the last remaining Russian and Polish ghettos. There were further arrivals of Western Jews, this time from Holland, Austria and even Germany. Whilst these new shipments brought temporary relief to Stangl and his SS personnel by keeping the camp going, the commandant knew that the shipments were not enough to sustain the camp's position for any appreciable length of time. In order to occupy his staff, and further justify their positions there, Stangl ordered the camp 'street' to be built, new fences to be erected, the forest cleared, and a zoo installed, where the SS could visit whilst off duty to relax. A young roe deer, two peacocks, and foxes were brought to the camp.

During these periods when the SS were off duty they regularly spent their time frequenting the local town or village bars or cafes, which was tolerated by their superiors. Generally though, the barracks and mess were where most personnel spent their time, eating, drinking and playing cards.

The bizarre construction of the zoo beside the Ukrainian barracks was intended to bring a kind of normality to daily life in the camp, but in reality it was only when they were physically removed from the camp that the guards were able to properly free their minds. Leave was always welcomed by the personnel, and yet for many travelling back to the homeland there was a growing fear that the war was being lost. This had diverse psychological effects on German citizens, but had its own meaning for those working in the death camps. They were harbouring a secret so terrible that all surely feared retribution if Germany lost the war. Yet, in order to justify their actions and remain posted to the camp they kept reassuring themselves that they were only following orders, and had sworn an oath of unconditional loyalty. Constantly they shielded themselves from taking responsibility for playing any part in the extermination process by insisting to themselves that 'they had been ordered to do it'. They also blamed the power of propaganda to which they were frequently exposed, and the effect of their nationalistic upbringing. There was growing anxiety about the future.

Although German radio relentlessly poured out news about the heroic fighting on the Eastern Front, many of the SS sitting in their barracks were not fooled by the propaganda. But despite the disasters in Russia, thanks to the zeal and effectiveness of the higher echelons of the SS, deportations of Jews were once again going very well. Auschwitz for one was running at full capacity, and would soon become the largest killing centre in the *Reich*. During March and April 1943, thousands of Dutch Jews were successfully transported to Sobibor, where they were immediately put to death. At Treblinka too the increase in shipments meant that the SS still had jobs and did not fear too much being sent to the front to fight in Russia. All now depended on proving themselves indispensable. Stangl knew that the only way to demonstrate the camp's worth as an effective killing factory was to continue to command it like a director managing production and distribution of a product. At the same time he knew that many thousands of Jews were being selected for labour. Treblinka was designed purely to kill. In other camps, only those designated in the main as 'unfit' for labour were being exterminated. Treblinka it seemed had reached its zenith, and now the camp was being run down before finally being forced to close for good.

During the third week of April news reached Treblinka that a few hundred Jews in Warsaw had organized an armed uprising. Fighting was so intense that the Germans were compelled to send in over 2,000 well-armed troops including *Waffen-SS Panzergrenadier* troops as well as a strong contingent of Polish police. Other detachments were embroiled in the fighting including a *Wehrmacht* anti-tank battery and a battalion of Ukrainian *Trawniki-Männer* from the Trawniki training camp. Ukrainian, Lithuanian and Latvian auxiliary policemen known as *Askaris* (Latvian *Arajs Kommando* and Lithuanian *Saugumas*), and technical emergency corps joined the task force to combat the uprising.

The fighting was relentless and it took some ten days before the Germans under the command of *SS-Brigadeführer* Jürgen Stroop could suppress the uprising, and the struggle continued into May. Approximately 13,000 Jews were killed in the ghetto during the uprising. Of the remaining 50,000 residents, most were captured and rounded up, destined for Treblinka.

When the first train load arrived from Warsaw, the SS personnel noticed that the box cars were in a terrible condition. According to one of the soldiers accompanying the train to the camp the prisoners inside the car, suspecting, perhaps knowing what awaited them, had frantically attempted to escape by pulling apart the wooden flooring and other internal fixings.

When the Jews were finally unloaded there was a sense of anxiety among the SS in the camp. Stangl had given his deputy strict instructions to move the Warsaw deportees through as quickly as possible to avoid panic and disorder. As they were unloaded under armed guard they were quickly escorted through to the square to be undressed. Whilst they undressed there was a sudden explosion, which wounded three prisoners and a few of the new arrivals. The SS men and the Ukrainian guards that had surrounded the square quickly bolted for cover, fearing there would be more explosions. After a few moments an alarm was raised and more guards came running to the square and quickly sealed off the area. It soon became apparent that the explosion had been a hand grenade hidden in the pocket of one of the Warsaw ghetto fighters.

Once the confusion had settled the Ukrainian guards under the supervision of the SS herded the deportees together. Those that were lying injured on the ground from the hand grenade explosion were shot, whilst the rest were led naked to the 'tube'. Many of them were kicked, punched and whipped as they were forced to run towards the gas chambers that lay beyond. *SS-Unterscharführer* Albert Franz Rum was one SS man that took great pride in chasing prisoners with whips to the gas chambers. He was also allocated as head of 'Sorting Barracks B' in the Sorting Yard, but spent considerable time as a guard for the Body-Transport Team in Camp II.

Once the deportees were herded into the chambers the steel airtight doors were slammed shut and bolted. Matthes and Münzberger could hear voices calling out, and people crying and scratching at the walls. They were totally unmoved by the noise, and called out to *SS-Unterscharführer* Fritz Schmidt who operated the gas chamber engines to start the motors and begin the gassing process. After the noise ceased, the SS waited for a few moments and then the doors were opened by members of the Body-Transport Team. They had to remove the bodies from the gas chamber and transport them to the 'roasters'. Once the chambers were empty they had to re-enter wielding powerful hoses to clean up the blood, urine and excrement that lay on the floors and over the walls. As for the SS, they stood around and smoked, chatting and joking with each other before preparing for the next shipment from Warsaw to arrive.

Whilst the systematic extermination of the Jews from the Warsaw uprising continued, a new policy at the camp was adopted. Stangl ordered that there would be no more selections of workers from new transports, and that all the *kommandos* that were regarded as no longer useful would be processed.

As the killings continued Stangl oversaw the modernizing and expanding of the camp. The zoo was still being erected by the prisoners, whilst additional work was undertaken on the Commandant's quarters. The main gate was rebuilt and the floor to the SS barracks was covered with carpet in an effort to muffle the sound of footsteps. In a room between two of the SS barracks was an arms store. For additional security a new reinforced steel door was delivered to the camp for the store. Outside the camp another railway line from Siedlce to Malkinia was constructed. At the station a double-track railway line was laid, and another bridge across the Bug River was constructed. For weeks gangs of labourers worked every day inside the camp, and along the railway lines that led to the Treblinka station. The SS were aware that in order for the camp to stay open it depended on new transports. The new rail line was one way of ensuring the camp remained functioning.

However, during late May anxiety once again mounted when the transports from the Warsaw ghetto begun drying up. The Jews working in the camp were also worried about the reduced transports, and feared for their lives.

Clearing of the ghettos in the General Government was virtually complete, and both Treblinka and Sobibor were receiving the last deliveries by early summer of 1943. Apart from the last Jews being delivered from Warsaw during this period the bulk of the shipments being received were now from Western Europe. But much to the consternation of the SS at Treblinka, many of the transports were now being directed to Auschwitz, where many of the healthy arrivals were being put to work. Other Jews left in the General Government were also being transferred to labour camps to help the war effort. From there Jews were hired out to firms, returning to the camps at night. Himmler, however, made it known that the employment of Jews would cease, even if they they were working in armaments factories.

In a meeting of the General Government the Higher SS and Police Leader, *SS-Gruppenführer* Walter Krüger, commented on the demand of the *Reichsführer*:

> Recently he was once again ordered to carry out the elimination of the Jews in a very short time. He was compelled to remove the Jews from the armaments industry and from our plants of military importance as well, unless they were exclusively employed in important work. The Jews were then concentrated in large camps and were being released from there each day for work in these armaments factories.
>
> However, the *Reichsführer SS* wishes that the employment of these Jews too should cease. He [Krüger] has discussed this question with Lieutenant General Schindler and considers that in the final analysis this wish of the *Reichsführer SS* probably cannot be fulfilled. Among the Jewish workers there are skilled workers, precision mechanics and other qualified craftsmen whom one could not easily replace with Poles. He therefore requests *SS-Obergruppenführer* Dr Kaltenbrunner to explain the situation to the *Reichsführer SS* and ask him to refrain from removing these Jewish workers.[41]

Despite this meeting of the SS of the General Government, the last ghettos in Poland continued to be dissolved at a tremendous rate and their inhabitants either exterminated or deported to the labour camps. The liquidation of the Warsaw ghetto had ensured that Treblinka would continue to function. This also included the cremation of the corpses, which were being burnt at a rate of some 84,000 a week. Once all traces of the crimes had finally been obliterated the camp would be dismantled and the SS personnel posted either to the front or other functioning camps.

Chapter V

End of Treblinka
(phase four)

By May 1943 Treblinka had entered the final stage in its operation as one of the main Reinhard camps. Transports continued to enter the camp bringing with them the last survivors of the rebellion of the Warsaw ghetto. Other trains that arrived were from the Russian and Polish ghettos, which were being cleared by special action squads during the *Wehrmacht's* slow retreat from Stalingrad. Others came from Holland and Austria and Germany.

Dealing with the German and Austrian Jews was the most difficult phase in the transition of Treblinka. Whilst the majority of SS personnel were not emotionally disturbed by these shipments from their country, some did not deal with it so easily. Stangl himself felt a kind of pity for his victims, especially German-speaking Jews, and felt he could never look one in the eye. He attempted to ignore the truth by trying to avoid witnessing the unloading of new arrivals, the beatings, shootings and the last journey of those who were sent through the 'tube' to the gas chambers. Other SS too were affected by the arrival of Western Jews, particularly from the Fatherland. They were of course able to identify with them much more easily than those from Poland and Russia, for their own lives had in some cases been similar. Unlike the Eastern Jews whose religious, racial and national feelings made for something approaching a single identity, and one which for centuries had been in part defined by the terror of pogroms, Western Jews were recognizably different, as they had not suffered to the same extent (at least in recent times). It was for this reason that the SS went to great lengths to mislead the Western Jews. Some of the box cars were made more presentable, in particular to convince the Jews from Germany and Austria that they were coming to be resettled. Their naivety was such that some on the transports actually offered tips to those who were unloading them.

When they arrived they were greeted at the ramp disguised as a railway station complete with flower beds. There were green fences, and normal looking barracks, and medical orderlies often lined up to 'care' for the 'old and sick'. There were polite voices telling them to disembark at their leisure, but in an orderly fashion. As they were unloaded off the train the SS were ordered not to use whips or unleash any type of physical abuse.

It was Suchomel who reported that Stangl, who was usually there on the ramp in his white suit, often on horseback, tried to avoid any transports from the West, especially if they came from Germany or Austria. Normally when German or Austrian Jews arrived in the camp they were accompanied by German police. The police officers were quickly ushered to the mess so that they did not witness the unloading. Once the Jews were out of sight and the box cars cleaned the police were hurried back onto the train out of Treblinka. As for the Jews, they were led through the camp quietly and kept calm until naked. It was only then that the deception would slip, as the SS and the Ukrainian guards escorted them to the 'tube' under the whip, hurling abuse and beating them often until they had been made physically and mentally incapable of resistance.

Stangl was not unduly concerned about the transition of the Jews once they were naked. It was only upon their initial arrival dressed in their best clothes with their luggage that they were identifiably Western Jews.

As for the Eastern Jew, the SS considereded that elaborate deception precautions were generally unnecessary for this 'subhuman species' for whom terror was a birthright. All the SS needed to do upon their arrival was to process them as quickly as possible. The moment the train stopped, Ukrainian guards lining the platform with the SS drawn up behind them deliberately provoked instant dread. As soon as the doors to the box cars were open the Ukrainians whipped the people out of the trains, shouting and screaming at them until the moment of their death. This difference of approach would become more clear-cut during the last phase of Treblinka, as more arrivals from the West came to be killed.

The early summer of 1943 had brought about an unusual atmosphere not experienced during the history of the camp's operation. This feeling was the direct result of the dire military situation on the Eastern Front and Himmler's insistence that Stangl hide the evidence of the slaughter. Whilst SS rules in the camp became more stringent than ever, some SS men were forcing themselves to be slightly more affable with the prisoners. Joe Siedlecki, who had worked at Treblinka as a gardener, said that although most of the SS treated the inmates like animals, some were actually genuinely good to them. But it is not difficult to conclude that the majority of the SS that did show signs of friendliness were planning to make use of individual prisoners who may one day speak in their defence if the war was lost. The system at Treblinka was still rigid as ever, and showing any kind of rapprochement with the prisoners was a dangerous game.

Throughout June the camp operated as normal, but never again would it see the volumes of shipments it received in late 1942. The SS went about their business with the same ruthlessness as before, but they seemed more composed and relaxed. When the heat was oppressive a number of them often took themselves off to bathe in the River Bug. Others basked in the sun outside their barracks, or decided to wander for long peaceful walks in the surrounding fields or woods, or visited the camp's zoo. Though there was definitely an underlying air of anxiety among the SS, the camp operated as efficiently as it had ever done under the command of Stangl. The Commandant was undoubtedly hard-pressed to maintain productivity in the camp, but he continued to liaise with his superiors in Lublin and Berlin regarding completing operations.

In July he went on leave and returned to his beloved wife and family for recuperation. His wife later said to Gitta Sereny that she had seen a terrible change in him.

No one else saw this. And I too had only glimpses; occasional glimpses of another man, somebody with a different, a totally changed face; someone I didn't know ... That was when I began to nag him – at least he called it that. I asked him again and again, 'Paul, why are you still there? It's a year now, more than a year. All the time you said you'd manage it, you'd wangle a transfer.' 'Paul,' I'd say, 'I'm afraid for you. I am afraid for your soul. You must leave. Run away if must be. We will come with you, anywhere.' 'How?' he said. 'They'd catch me. They catch everybody. And that would be the end for all of us' ... I could no longer be with him ... you know ... near him. It was quite terrible, for both of us. We were staying in the mountains with this friend of my mother's, a priest, Father Mario; she had arranged for us to stay there, for our holiday. And one day I couldn't stand it any longer; I no longer knew where to turn, I had to talk to somebody. So I went to see Father Mario. I said, 'Father, I must talk to you. I want to talk under the seal of the confessional'... I told him about Treblinka. I said, 'I know you won't believe it but there is a terrible place in Poland and they are killing people there, they are killing Jews there. What shall I do?' Father Mario said 'we are living through terrible times, my child. Before God and my conscience, if I had been in Paul's place, I would have done the same. I absolve him from all guilt.' ... The priest had taken it so ... not calmly, but, well, matter-of-factly. I don't know. I could no longer think at all. And that night, I told Paul that I had told Father Mario and what he had answered. All Paul said was, 'You took a terrible risk telling him.' He wasn't angry, he didn't rave at me like I thought he might. I think I was grateful for that. I had been so lonely and frightened ... Well, his leave came to an end soon after that.[42]

Life for Stangl, and indeed many of the SS personnel that were at Treblinka during the summer months of 1943, consisted of living a life of relative ease on the one hand, and experiencing a growing sense of foreboding on the other. There were SS men like Kurt Franz who attempted to distract themselves by implementing various activities, such as boxing matches among the prisoners. Franz had been an amateur boxer himself, and was regularly seen training. Often he would be seen hitting the prisoners. Now he could use his knowledge of the sport as another means to torture the prisoners – much to the delight of the SS spectators. During the spring and early summer he put together a group of prisoners and made them practise boxing.

Every two weeks on Saturday afternoon a ring was erected in the Roll-Call square in the prisoners' living area. The SS sat around the ring on chairs, whilst Kapos, work managers and the women sat on benches at the side. The matches were opened by Gold's orchestra, followed by artists that told jokes and performed humorous sketches. The whole event was bizarre beyond the surreal.

The first matches began with boxers that fought to a high standard, but Franz was not entertained by this and demanded that normal prisoners who had no idea how to box were to fight in the ring. The SS spectators enjoyed the fighting and loudly urged the two prisoners press-ganged into the ring to hit each other.

Apart from the twice-monthly boxing matches, the SS also came up with the idea of putting on a play in order to keep the prisoners busy and the guards amused. Preparations were made and even some professional actors were found to rehearse and then star in the performances. In the corridors of the gas chambers prisoners were taught to dance the minuet – that pretty, delicate, ceremonious dance for two – and the czardas, a traditional Hungarian folk dance. A stage was built in the Roll-Call square. The play was held one Sunday, much to the delight of the SS who occupied all the front row seats for the event.

The play was a great success, and for a time whilst the prisoners performed on the stage it must have been a kind of release for them, however brief, however absurd, from the the executions, the daily beatings, torture and the debilitating work. The play was another example of the unreal world that the SS were building for themselves. They continued to keep their family and loved ones ignorant. It was not only the secrecy rule that prevented them from telling anyone about Treblinka, but also because they were dependent on their families' approval of them as husband, father, provider, a professional success – and also as a dignified man who was respected. As SS men they had persuaded themselves that the extermination of the Jewish race was justifiable, and if a family member made the occasional remark about the shipment of the Jews it must have been difficult for them. To avoid facing the truth, they said nothing about their real task, only reiterating what they had been told when they first arrived at Treblinka – that they had been transferred to a special job to oversee Jews at a camp.

As long as the SS could hide the truth from the outside world and win the war, then they did not need to worry about retribution. Yet, however optimistic the average SS man was in the summer months of 1943, he could not deny the fact that the German war machine was breaking down on the Eastern Front. By the end of July the *Wehrmacht* had had lost its will to advance. It was being sucked into a long, bitter struggle for survival. With a string of defeats in its wake the German Army were now withdrawing across a bombed and blasted Soviet landscape, with little hope of holding back the Red Army. The summer campaign in Russia had been completely disastrous. Against overwhelmingly superior forces the Germans had withdrawn some 150 miles along a 650-mile front. Slowly but defiantly they retreated, always outnumbered, constantly low on fuel, ammunition and other supplies. To make matters worse partisans added another dimension to the war in Russia. Knowing of the inexorable advance of the Soviet Army, Ukrainian nationalist partisans, communist partisans and Polish underground groups began raiding German outposts, barracks, police stations, supply dumps, rail depots and trains.

Despite the deteriorating military situation Himmler and his 'Reinhard' leaders were still consumed with a desire to finish what they had begun. The *Reichsführer* could follow his impulses in the knowledge that Globocnik and Wirth were right behind him. They had nearly succeeded in exterminating the Jews in the General Government and were now in the final process of decommissioning Sobibor and Treblinka. Every effort had been made by Himmler's office in Berlin to avoid disrupting the war effort by trying to complete the last shipments to the death camps as quickly as possible. The remaining Jewish prisoners in the camp had been told that they had to work well, and they would be treated fairly. Stangl made it known that the prisoners had to believe that nothing was being demanded of them except discipline and order. He told Franz that he wanted the Jews to know they had nothing to fear and that he wanted to avoid violence, but this was only possible if they cooperated. Upon Stangl's return from leave at the end of July he devoted much of his time to secret briefings and working out the last phase of the camp with his subordinates. The major deportations from Western Europe had virtually ground to a halt, and there were no more than small-scale hunts for the last remaining Jews in the General Government. The SS in Treblinka tried their best to adhere to their commandant's requests and treat the prisoners with less vehemence. As a consequence, some of the prisoners become individuals of sorts to them, and a terrible new kind of community of murderers and victims began to flourish. But this was once again a strategy of deception; Stangl saw the potential in lulling the prisoners into complacency about their imprisonment. The SS had become masters of trickery, and the new approach had been implemented in order to get the job completed at the camp in the shortest possible time and without the prisoners suspecting that they would be killed once they were no longer required.

Stangl was determined to run an efficient camp right to the end. He had set up a well-organized office, recruited subordinates wisely, and had created a very good relationship with his superiors. He stayed in touch with his representatives in Lublin by visiting them regularly, and this became more frequent during the summer months of 1943. By these means he was able to manage the camp and keep it operating under difficult conditions. The running of the camp had been complex, even for a natural administrator like Stangl. Contrary to popular belief the process of killing hundreds of thousands of people had been riddled with inconsistencies and contradictions, and the work was actually poorly resourced. It had therefore been left to people like Stangl to improvise the machinery of murder. Stangl often despaired at the inconsistencies of policy. The biggest headache had been the task of exhuming almost 800,000 corpses from the burial pits. By the end of July 1943 there were some 200,000 corpses left to be burned. All traces of extermination in the camp were to be obliterated with the utmost speed. A staff officer attached to Wirth's office wrote:

I frequently visited TII in the summer of 1943 and regularly reported back to Wirth with a progress report on the dismantling of the camp. Whilst the commandant [Stangl] was on leave I came to Treblinka and was given a guided tour by Deputy Franz and another officer. Here I was shown the cremation areas and the pits where the corpses were being exhumed by prisoners. I had my briefcase with me and I got my assistant to write down notes on the calculation Franz gave me on the total number of bodies exhumed thus far. I was not chiefly interested in the quantity or condition of the prisoners working inside these pits, but more anxious about how the job was going to be completed in the specified time.[43]

Whilst the roasters burned all day and all night, Franz ordered stones, concrete and other building materials to be brought in to help burn the remaining corpses. Treblinka in the summer of 1943 had become a huge crematorium.

July was coming to an end. The days were sweltering, scorching. The hardest work was at the graves, because of the stench ... Seventy-five per cent of the victims had already been burnt. Now the ground had to be flattened and the area tidied ... The new work started as the empty graves had to be filled up ... The empty area had to be used. It was surrounded with a fence of barbed wire. A stretch of land belonging to the other camp was attached. An attempt to plant something in this area was made.

The soil turned out to be fertile. The gardeners planted lupins with great success.[44]

SS-Scharführer Herbert Floss had made a name for himself as the *Aktion Reinhard* cremation expert at Belzec, Sobibor and Treblinka, and was commander of Camp II. He was in charge of the arrangements for cremating the corpses, and was nicknamed '*Tadellos'* (perfect) by the 'Jewish Death Brigade' he commanded, as he would often say 'Thank God, now the fire's perfect.'

Floss was generally regarded by his fellow comrades as a quiet, sincere man, who excelled in his job. A Staff officer named Kratzer visiting Treblinka with one of Globocnik's representatives found Floss to be a 'determined fellow' who displayed versatility 'and much relish for the mission'. Kratzer went on to write in his diary:

> I admire the way in which our men are dealing with cremating the corpses. I have been informed from the cremation expert Floss that the burnings will be terminated by the end of August or September ... There is much activity in the camp and the staff here are working exceptionally hard to bring about a conclusion to this dirty work. TII is certainly being run effectively and my report on its decommissioning will be presented in due course.[45]

Kratzer spent a day at Treblinka some time at the end of July or early August 1943. He toured the camp with a number of other officers, who had more than likely come from the 'Reinhard' headquarters in Lublin. He visited the 'Upper Camp' and saw for himself the gas chambers, the installations for the disposal of the corpses and the huge iron roasters, and the barracks for the Jewish work-groups. Both males and females worked in this area – the men carried and burned the bodies, whilst the women cooked and washed. In the 'Lower Camp' he saw the unloading ramp and the square where the selections were made. He saw the fake hospital, the *Lazarett*, the undressing barracks, and then went to see the 'road to heaven'. He visited the living and working quarters of the Jewish workers who staffed the lower part of the camp: the joiners, shoe-makers, goldsmiths, carpenters, kitchen hands, doctors in the clinic and the Kapos. To the right of this he was taken to see what the SS nicknamed the 'ghetto' complex – the yard where roll-call was

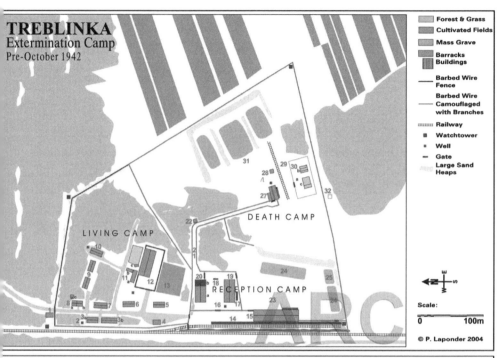

TREBLINKA
Extermination Camp
Pre-October 1942

Forest & Grass
Cultivated Fields
Mass Grave
Barracks
Buildings
Barbed Wire
Fence
Barbed Wire
Camouflaged
with Branches
Railway
Watchtower
Well
Gate
Large Sand
Heaps

DEATH CAMP

LIVING CAMP

RECEPTION CAMP

Scale:
0   100m

© P. Laponder 2004

KEY:

An 1940 aerial photo was used to fill in detail of forest in camp.
The original Wiernik map was used for the Tube and change of fencing in middle of camp.
The anti tank trap fencing was erected later etc.

Some reasons for placing features are mentioned in italics.

LIVING CAMP
1 First guard house. *(Was first outside gate and removed when Tyrolean guard house was build inside fence. The ornate main gate was built only later)*
2 Officer's well.
3 SS living quarters: a. Mess, b. Sleeping quarters.
4 Garage. *(Probably the garage shed was first at this side)*
5 Food Store. *(Probably later removed when big shed was built in sorting yard)*
6 Old Bakery.
7 Store for sorting valuables. *(Probably later became SS service building)*
8 a. Camp Commandant's living quarters b. Administrative office b. Punishment cell for Ukrainians.
9 Living quarters for Ukrainians. *(A few survivor maps [including Glazar's] indicate these barracks in this layout, it could well have been an earlier layout)*
10 Ukrainian kitchen.
11 Farmyard area: a. Stables, b. Pigsty, c. Chicken run.

12 Barrack for *Hofjuden, Goldjuden* sorting room and workshops. *(The other barracks were later build forming the 'U' shaped 'Gheto' complex)*
13 Vegetable garden. *(It is probable that a vegetable garden was turned into a Roll Call area. [The Platkiewickz map shows a vegetable garden in this area.]. The original Roll Call area was on the ramp in front of the undressing barracks)*

RECEPTION CAMP
STATION SQUARE
14 Platform for victim disembarkation and original Roll-Call area for prisoners. *(As mentioned in unpublished Strawcsynski memoirs).*
15 Storage barracks for items taken away from victims.

DEPORTATION SQUARE
16 Separation of victims: women to the left, men to the right
17 Open pit toilet. *(Later removed).*
18 Notice board, informing victims what to do. *(Later removed).*
19 Barracks. *(First used for male sleeping quarters later a wood store).*
20 a. Undressing barracks for females, b. Barber section *(Probable that the barber section was later added. Survivor Bomba [a barber] testifies that originally the cutting was done in the Old Gaschambers!!)*
21 'The Tube'. *(Note the original long length and the fact that the tube ran in a straight line towards the entrance of the Old Gas Chambers. The New Gas Chambers were built to make use of the same position of the Tube. There is evidence that the Old*

Gas Chamber entrance lines up with the centre passage of the New Gas Chambers)
22 Kiosk for collecting valuables from victims going through 'The Tube'. *(Later removed as it hampered the speedy flow of victims to gas chambers)*

SORTING AREA
23 Sorting Yard. *(Probably the Latrines were build later. Double Barracks not included probably build later although Willenberg writes they were originally farm stables. Cannot be identified on 1940 aerial)*
24 Mass graves. *(Where corpses were buried during initial hectic phase as evident on aerial photo)*
25 Part of original mass grave which was later the site of the Lazarett.

DEATH CAMP
26 Old gas chambers. *(The original three smaller gas chambers)*
27 Guard house. *(Probably there from the beginning)*
28 Narrow gauge railway. *(Later removed as it was impractical and the rails were used to make experimental cremation grids)*
29 Sonderkommando camp. *(The middle section of the barracks seems to have been build later as the Wiernik model indicates it as two separate barracks)*
30 No mass graves here yet. *(The earth mound being formed by the mass graves in the sorting yard. According to Wiernik's map, there were only mass graves in the east side of the camp)*
31 Mass graves.
32 Watchtower. *(Originally in this position but later removed to centre of Death Camp).*

TREBLINKA MAP (PRE-OCTOBER 1942)
This is probably the first map of the camp in which the features are drawn to scale (as near as possible) and the actual shape and size of the camp are attempted. The map is intended to show how the camp was in a constant state of development and improvement. Although the map was drawn taking several testimonies into consideration, it is not necessarily an accurate record. Copyright: P. Laponder. (Courtesy of ARC)

taken twice a day. Here he saw the ghetto-latrine, which the work Jews could only visit for a specified number of minutes and was controlled by a prisoner guard dressed by the SS as a rabbi, and called the 'shit-master'.

To the left of this central area, beyond another fence, were the quarters for the 80 Ukrainian guards. From here Kratzer and his small delegation were led along the 'Kurt-Seidel Strasse' which was flanked on either side with beautiful flowers and shrubs. South-east of this road he was brought to Stangl's quarters, which contained his bedroom, his study, a guest room, and the offices of his two administrative assistants, the book-keeper Matzig, and the orderly Stadie. Here there was an SS dentist, clinic for the staff, barbers, and the camp zoo. Across the street there were the SS living quarters where 40 men could be housed, but there were only 20 stationed there at any one time. Kratzer wrote:

> After my tour I made specific notes and a sketch of the camp so that my boss had an overall idea of the general layout of the camp. This was undertaken in order to make preparations for the installation's decommissioning.[46]

Stangl did not meet Kratzer or his delegation as he was probably still on leave. In any case, he had always been uneasy about admitting any officers, even from the Lublin headquarters, but he did authorize visitors to see just his headquarters, or the SS mess. By this time,

> … after eleven or so in the morning, nothing really went on except routine work in the work-shops. Of course up in the top camp they'd have their fires – they'd burn what was left over; there was always something going on there.[47]

Stangl had tried his utmost to keep the camp as secret as possible from the outside world, but villages and farms in the surrounding area all knew about Treblinka. Stangl:

> Hundreds of soldiers and civilians used to come up to our gate, stand along the fences, gawk, and try to buy things off us because it was known that there was all this stuff around. For a while we even had planes circling around overhead and flying low so that they could watch what was going

on. I rang through to HQ about that finally and they told us to shoot at them. So we did, and that stopped that. But we never could stop the others – not quite, ever. They saw dead Jews on the ground and being carried away from the station. They photographed them. The whole place stank to high heaven from kilometres away. For two weeks after coming through there – or 'visiting' there – many used to say they couldn't eat.[48]

Stangl arrived back in the camp from leave on Sunday 1 August. The following day had always been a day of rest at the camp as there were no transports because nobody worked in Warsaw on Sunday loading the trains. Even by early August with all the Jews removed from Warsaw the SS still used Mondays as an opportunity to relax. Stangl remembered that

> … Kurt Franz had taken a swimming party of twenty down to the River Bug straight after lunch; four Germans and the rest of the Ukrainians. I had a visitor, a Viennese. He was an army political officer who was temporarily stationed in Kossov, six kilometres away. He had rung to say hello and ask whether he could drop by.

According to Suchomel, Matzig was also present with the commandant and his friend, and all three men drank a considerable amount of alcohol that Monday afternoon. According to Suchomel 'Stangl and his friend were both drunk as lords and didn't know which end was up.' Suddenly, at around 2pm Stangl heard some shooting coming from a blockhouse.

> My batman, Sacha, he was Ukrainian, he came running. Looking out of my window I could see some Jews on the other side of the fence – they must have jumped down from the roof of the SS billets and they were shooting. I told the fellow from Kossov to stay put and took my pistol and ran out. By that time the guards had begun to shoot back but there were already fires all over the camp.[49]

What followed was utter confusion in the camp as gun shots were fired, and grenades and bottles of petrol exploded, setting fire to some of the buildings. What made it more difficult to suppress the revolt immediately was the fact that Stangl's deputy Franz and two-thirds of the camp personnel had gone swimming. Even the guard in the watch tower, called Mira, had been caught unawares sunning himself, dressed only in his shorts. He was quickly roused by the sound of gun shots from the lower camp and jumped down. Almost immediately he was overpowered by a Jew. According to Stangl:

> At the moment of the revolt we had about 840 Jews in the upper and lower camp. When the shooting stopped, after about ten minutes, we called out that those who wanted our protection were to assemble outside my quarters … more than 100 reported to us when we called.[50]

The remainder were either hiding, fearing they would be killed in the cross fire, had been shot by the guards, or had fled into the surrounding forests. Troops immediately surrounded the camp at a distance of five kilometres, and the SS issued an order to the local Polish population informing them that Jews had escaped from the camp infected with typhus, and that helping them would be punishable by death. Posters warned of the escape of 50 Jewish bandits, but the figure was more like 100.

The revolt caused consternation among the staff of Operation Reinhard in Lublin. Globocnik and Wirth were incensed and considered closing down the camp immediately. However, Globocnik decided that considering there were no casualties, the camp could still continue to function and a report did not need to be filed to Himmler in Berlin. Suchomel:

> After the revolt and all the fires, of all things the gas chambers remained intact, they were of brick. And Stangl said to me, 'The fools, why didn't they burn those down?' … Stangl was going to put the work-Jews to work outside the camp, in the peat bog; the new programme was to start on 3 August, one day after the revolt. He intended to rebuild Treblinka, better than ever; he was going to have brick houses for the work-Jews. He already had building materials lying there all ready when the order came to obliterate the camp.[51]

When Franz and his SS comrades returned to the camp they were shocked by the sight that greeted them. The SS barracks was smouldering, the gas chambers dark with smoke, and other buildings also had extensive fire damage including the railway station installation. Parts of the outer fence had been blown open and there were the bodies strewn everywhere of those who had been gunned down whilst trying to escape.

Out of the 840 Jewish prisoners in the camp it had been estimated that only around 150 of them had not attempted to escape, too sick or frightened to leave the camp. About 600 of them died in the camp or in the surrounding woods and countryside, whilst 100 prisoners actually succeeded in breaking out to the forests.

Franz was incensed by the revolt and wanted to shoot every prisoner, but Stangl forbade such an action and wanted to interrogate them. He was shocked by the uprising and feared he would be made wholly accountable.

Over the next few weeks, however, Stangl heard nothing from his superiors about the uprising, and continued to operate the camp as best he could. On 18 August came transports from the Bialystock ghetto, which consisted of 37 cars. Stangl had received word that over 25,000 Jews from the ghetto were destined for Treblinka, and was concerned because the camp was far from fully operational. There were only a handful of Jews left after the uprising and Stangl was deeply troubled that the killing process would be hindered by delays. Only ten of the cars could now enter the camp simultaneously, instead of the previous twenty. The Commandant contacted the Lublin headquarters and told them that because Treblinka had ceased to be fully operational shipments would have to be significantly reduced temporarily until further measures were implemented. He soon received an answer from HQ, telling him that other transports would be redirected.

The following day came another transport from Bialystock, this time with 39 cars. The other three transports, two of which that had been originally earmarked for Treblinka, were re-directed. One was destined for Auschwitz, the other to Majdanek, and one to Theresienstadt, which contained a consignment of children.

The murder of the Bialystock Jews took a considerable time, and as a consequence many remained locked in the box cars for hours waiting to die. Conditions in the cars quickly deteriorated. Many, especially children, became filthy and their clothes were soiled. The old and the sick died of dehydration. Those that remained alive stood crammed together, gasping for air through the slats of the car.

When they were eventually unloaded there was widespread relief. But this was short-lived as the selection process separated men from women, husbands from wives, and resulted in many emotional disturbances. Particular efforts were made to reassure the Jews, because more than ever it was in the interests of the SS to keep them as calm as possible – they knew that they lacked sufficient numbers of personnel and workers to deal with the transports.

The following day saw another transport from Bialystock arrive, 39 wagons. Unbeknown to Stangl, transport 'PJ-204' would be the last shipment of Jews to Treblinka. All the remaining trains bypassed the camp bound for Majdanek and Sobibor.

A few days following the liquidation of the Bialystock ghetto, Stangl was finally summoned by Globocnik to the Lublin HQ:

As soon as I entered the office Globocnik said, 'You are transferred immediately to Trieste for anti-partisan combat.' I thought my bones would melt. I had been so sure they'd say I had done something wrong, and now I had on the contrary what I had always wanted; I was going to get out. And to Trieste too – near home.

I went back to Treblinka, but I only stayed three or four days. Just long enough to organize transport. The last day I had all the work-Jews who were left fall in, because I wanted to say goodbye to them. I shook hands with some of them.[52]

Suchomel noticed how overjoyed Stangl was that he was finally leaving for a new posting in Italy.

As Stangl packed the last of his belongings in his quarters Jewish workers were removing everything from the special storage facilities, and loading them on single wagons. As with all camps in the Nazi Empire, foreign currency, valuables, gold and other precious metals were to be transported to the SS headquarters in Berlin. Usable clothing, shoes, bed linen, blankets, fabrics, and household utensils were to be directed to the Ethnic German Liaison Office and distributed for the use of German settlers. As for unusable clothing and other pieces of material, these were to be sent directly to the Reich Ministry of Economy and used for the war effort. A Jewish worker named Zabecki wrote:

Such wagons left the camp on 2, 9, 13 and 21 September … On 30 September, the German railway man, Rudolf Emmerich, who was employed to watch the transports entering the camp, left the Treblinka station and went to Warsaw.[53]

With Stangl's departure from the camp Globocnik appointed Kurt Franz commander of Treblinka, and he was made responsible for dismantling the camp, destroying the gas chambers and removing any trace of the crimes committed there. There were several SS personnel at Franz's disposal and a group of Ukrainian guards. Much of the dismantling of the camp was undertaken by the remaining Jewish workers.

Between September and October all wooden buildings were disassembled, and anything that could be reused was loaded onto waiting trains. Everything was carefully dismantled, even down to removing the concrete foundations. Wooden fences and barbed wire were also taken down and brick buildings removed and taken away. Some of the materials were transported to the work camp Treblinka I, including the anti-tank obstacles. Zabecki:

> At the beginning of October, it was noticed at the station in Treblinka that elements of disassembled barracks, wooden planks, chlorinated lime … were being shipped out of the death camp. Later, the digger-dredger machine which was no longer needed was taken away.[54]

On 21 October the engines that fed the gas chambers were removed and transported by rail to Lublin. Other materials including bricks, wood, window frames, roofing, were also shipped out by rail. This included furniture, and other interior items. Important documents and files, including communiqués, left for Lublin in a convoy of vehicles under armed escort, and anything that was regarded as incriminating evidence was ordered to be burned.

Throughout the remaining part of October and the rest of November the liquidation of the camp continued. On 20 November transport wagons Nos 22757, 22536, 70136 and 139789, were shipped out to Sobibor. During this period over 100 wagons full of equipment left Treblinka.

Only a handful of SS personnel now remained behind to oversee the dismantling operation. The 30 Jewish workers that were now left were living in two railway wagons. The remainder of the prisoners in Treblinka at about this time, around 70 of them, had been liquidated. Among the survivors were two women working in the kitchen on a nearby farm where some of the Ukrainian guards had taken up residence.

On 16 November an order came through from Lublin that all personnel be removed from Treblinka, and that the remaining prisoners be put to

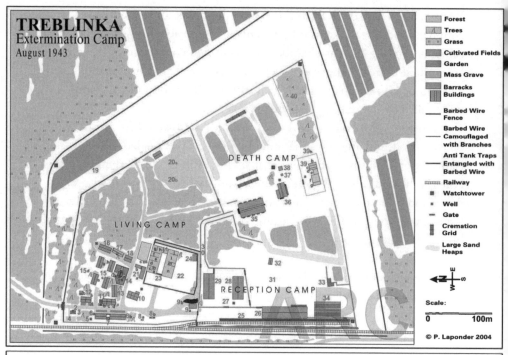

KEY:

LIVING CAMP

1 Main gate.
2 Tyrolean guard house.
3 Armoured car. (used for transporting to Lublin, valuables taken from victims)
4 SS relaxation area.
5 Officer's well.
6 SS living quarters: a. Mess b. Sleeping quarters.
7 Arms storeroom and water tower.
8 a. Petrol tank b. Petrol pumps.
9 a. Garage b. Coal dump.
10 New bakery foundations. (utilized later for 'farmhouse' housing an Ukrainian, guarding against locals plundering mass graves)
11 Service building for the SS: a. Air raid shelter, b. Sick bay c. Dentist d. Barber.
12 a. Camp commandant's office and living quarters, b. Wine & spirits cellar.
13 Staff sleeping quarters for Polish and Ukrainian girls.
14 Zoo area; a. Zoo with pigeon coop on top b. Relaxation area for SS.
15 Living quarters for Ukrainians: a. Sleeping quarters, b. Night shift quarters c. Doctor and barber d. Roll call and exercise area for Ukrainians.
16 Ukrainian kitchen.
17 Potato cellars.
18 GoldJuden. (Where Jewish prisoners had to sort valuables and gold taken from victims)

19 Vegetable garden.
20 a. Timber store & yard b. Waste combustion area.
21 Farmyard area: a. Stables b. Pigsty, c. Chicken run etc.

ROLL-CALL SQUARE

22 Assembly area for prisoners.
23 'The Ghetto': Jewish prisoners' living and working quarters: a. Jewish kitchen, b. SS laundry, c. Jewish infirmary, d. Kapo barrack, e. Saddlery and shoemaker shop, f. Tailor shop, g. Jewish women's quarters, H. Carpenter shop, i. Blacksmith & locksmith, j. Tool storehouse, k. Jewish quarters I, l. Washroom m. Jewish quarters II.
24 Latrines.

RECEPTION CAMP

STATION SQUARE

25 Platform for victim disembarkation (accommodating 20 cattle trucks).
26 Storage barracks for items taken away from victims (Disguised at a later stage, on the platform side, as a railway station called Obermaidan, with a fake ticket window and locked doors with signs such as 'To first-class waiting room')

DEPORTATION SQUARE

27 Separation of victims: women to the left, men to the right.
28 Barracks (First served as male sleeping quarters, later a lumber store)

29 Undressing barracks for females (Including a 'cash-desk' and an area where barbers had to cut the prisoners' hair).
30 'The Tube' (Narrow camouflaged passage called the Himmelstrasse (road to heaven) through which victims were chased to 'the showers').

SORTING AREA

31 Sorting Yard.
32 Latrine.
33 Lazarett (field hospital), an execution site disguised as a hospital.
34 Double Barracks (For victims' belongings already sorted).

DEATH CAMP

35 New gas chambers (Five steps with potted plants leading up to entrance and passage. Ten gas chambers, each hermetically sealed, opened via trapdoors onto platforms outside, from which the corpses were removed)
36 Old gas chambers (The original three smaller Gas chambers).
37 Water pump shelter.
38 Guard house.
39 Sonderkommando camp (prisoners working in death camp section): a. Roll-call yard, b. Woman's quarters, c. Doctor, d. Kapo, e. Ablution, f. Men's Quarters, g. Kitchen, h. Laundry area.
40 Concealed burial pit (Re-vegetated with saplings and lupine).

TREBLINKA MAP (AUGUST 1943)

This is another attempt to draw the features to scale and the actual shape and size of the camp are taken in consideration. But this redrawn map should by no means be considered as an exact representation of the camp – that would never be possible. There are simply too many discrepancies in all of the maps and witness reports. Copyright: P. Laponder. (Courtesy of ARC) death. This was left in the capable hands of Kurt Franz. He rounded up the Jews, and with the aid of the Ukrainian guards brought in from the work camp, they were herded into the railway wagons. *SS-Unterscharführer* Bredow then went to the kitchens to collect the two women there, and led them out. Willy Mentz, Bredow, and an unknown SS-man holding the rank of an *SS-Unterführer* from camp I carried out the executions. After the first group had been executed, the railway wagons were opened and five men were led out and ordered to carry the corpses of the women to a stake prepared earlier by the Ukrainians. Here the men were told to kneel down, and were shot in the back of the head. This process was repeated a number of times until all the prisoners were dead. It was left to the Ukrainian guards to ensure that all the corpses were burned to ashes, and traces of the crime completely removed. These victims were the last Jews to be murdered at Treblinka. Once the executions had taken place, Franz, together with Bredow and Mentz, bade farewell to the *SS-Unterführer* from Camp I.

On 17 November, the last Ukrainian guard departed from Treblinka for Lublin. The following day Kurt Franz requested that one of his subordinates take his dog Barry to his friend in Ostrow. As for Franz and the rest of the remaining SS personnel, they hitched a lift to Sobibor, whilst the last train departed from Treblinka carrying the final pieces of equipment from the camp.

On the ground where the death camp once stood there were still traces of barbed wire, heaps of earth and sand, some pits, and various pieces of material lying around. A building firm was immediately brought in to construct a farm house on top of the existing site using the bricks from the gas chambers. Once this had been hastily built, livestock was brought in and a Ukrainian by the name of Strebel who had been a guard in Treblinka was asked to live there and farm the land with his family. Strebel ensured that no trace of the camp existed and went to work ploughing the land, sowing lupins and planting pine woods where some 800,000 souls had been murdered at the hands of the SS.

Epilogue

With the liquidation of Treblinka *Aktion Reinhard* was almost at an end. For his accomplishment in wiping out nearly every Jew in the General Government Globocnik was promoted and appointed by Himmler as the Higher SS and Police Leader in the Trieste area in the north-east of Italy. Globocnik left Lubin in September 1943 and took with him Wirth and Stangl. He also brought along with him a number of other SS men from Treblinka, some of whom followed on later. They included Kurt Franz, Paul Bredow, Johannes Eisold, Willy Grossmann, August Hengst, Otto Horn, Hermann Lambert, Artur Matthes, Willy Matzig, Wilhelm Miete, Max Moller, Gustav Munzberger, Karl-Heinz Plikat, Paul Rost, Franz-Albert Rum, Karl Schiffner, Fritz Schmidt, Otto Stadie, and Franz Suchomel.

Stangl wrote about his new posting to Trieste:

> My first assignment in Trieste and for the first three months, to December, was 'Transport Security'. I realized quite well, and so did most of us, that they wanted to 'incinerate' us. So that we were assigned the most dangerous jobs – anything to with anti-partisan combat in that part of the world was very perilous.[55]

Whilst the new posting to Trieste was indeed a dangerous assignment, Stangl was relieved to have left Treblinka behind. A few weeks later in October 1943, Sobibor too was shut down and the buildings along with the gas chambers erased. With the liquidation of the 'Reinhard' camps it was left to other installations such as Auschwitz to carry on with the systematic annihilation of Europe's Jews.

Though the SS had been determined to remove all traces of the 'Reinhard' camps, once the job had been completed, they also wanted to be praised for the great service they had performed in completing the near extinction of the Jews in the General Government.

On 4 November, Globocnik wrote to Himmler:

On 19 October 1943 I concluded the 'Reinhard Action' which I have been carrying out in the General Government and dissolved all the camps ... As a final report I have taken the liberty of sending you the enclosed file, *Reichsführer*. My observations in Lublin have shown that there was a particular source of infection in the General Government, but particularly in the district of Lublin and so I endeavoured to produce a graphic record of these threats. If may prove useful in future to be able to draw attention to this threat. On the other hand, I have attempted to provide a description of the work involved from which one can see not only the amount of work but also with how few Germans this major action could be carried out. At any rate, it has now increased to such an extent that renowned industries are showing an in interest in it. In the meantime, I have handed over these camps to SS *Obergruppenführer* Pohl.

I would be grateful, *Reichsführer*, if you would peruse this file.

During a visit, *Reichsführer*, you indicated to me that, after the conclusion of the work, some Iron Crosses could be awarded for the particular achievements involved in this difficult work. I would be grateful if you could let me know if I may put forward recommendations.

I would like to take the liberty of pointing out that such awards were made to the forces of the SS and Police Leader who was involved in the Warsaw operation, which represented a relatively small part of the whole project.

I would be grateful to you, *Reichsführer*, for a positive decision in this matter since I like to see the hard work of my men rewarded.[56]

On 30 November 1943, Himmler replied to Globocnik's letter:

Dear Globus,

I confirm receipt of your letter of 4 November 1943, and your report
of the conclusion of the 'Reinhard Action'. I also am grateful to you for
sending me the file.

I would like to express to you my thanks and appreciation for the great
and unique service which you have preformed for the whole German
people by carrying out the 'Reinhard Action'.[57]

The SS felt they had completed a satisfactory job, and some were
rewarded for their efforts. They had convinced themselves that the Jew
was a racial-biological threat and a political enemy. Furthermore, they had
seen first-hand how the Jews had transformed themselves into terrorists
and partisans. The Warsaw ghetto uprising and then the Jewish revolt in
Treblinka reinforced the conviction that it was necessary to wipe them out.
Yet, as we have seen in this volume, off duty many of the SS-men were
such ordinary people. How could it be possible that such ordinary men
knowingly perpetrated such atrocities? Firstly, they were able to bury their
emotions and any possible revulsion at committing atrocities because the
Jews were regarded as 'the enemy', and had no intrinsic claim to life. Though
some struggled psychologically with the daily duties of murder, as we have
seen they could have easily been replaced by someone else. They stayed on
as obedient subordinates and continued to try and prove themselves worthy.
At Treblinka, some of the SS were not ideologically motivated, they were
not Nazi fanatics. The job to them was simply a way to succeed within the
SS order.

The capture, trial and execution of a number of the perpetrators after the
war reminded every country in Europe that it was touched by the Final
Solution. The terrible deeds of men like Wirth and Stangl at Treblinka made
them an example of the worst of Nazism. They sent more than 800,000
people to their death, though the figure is much lower than Wirth would
have wanted. It had become the second largest killing centre in the Nazi
regime, and would have exceeded the death toll of Auschwitz if it had
remained fully operational through 1944. The SS had not only 'cleansed' the
General Government in just over one year but incredibly kept the erection
of the camp and the activities there secret from the overwhelming majority
of victims.

When the Red Army marched through Treblinka in the summer of 1944 they were told about the murders, the burying of the bodies and the burning of the corpses. They had heard stories that there were great treasures hidden in the ground with the dead. These rumours were more than enough to bring masses of people to the area with spades and shovels to start digging and searching. In an attempt to find at least one gold tooth from the ground they dug a number of pits in the predominantly sandy soil. The looting continued for some years until the Polish Government decided to turn the former camp into a national memorial site.

Today a huge concrete memorial stands where the Treblinka camp once stood. The memorial bears witness to the massacres that were carried out on the site. The killers had done exceedingly well to remove all evidence of mass murder, but their hope that their crimes had been concealed forever was in vain.

Appendix I

List of SS Commandants, Officers and Guards

Inspector of *Aktion Reinhard* Death Camps

WIRTH, Christian *SS-Sturmbannführer* SS-Number: 345 464
24/11/1885–26/05/1944
Inspector of all *Aktion Reinhard* death camps, and commander of the DAW
(Deutsche Ausrüstungswerke) at Lublin Airfield. Following the euthanasia
T-4 programme in September 1941 he was ordered to join the staff of
SS- und Polizeiführer im Distrikt Lublin Odilo Globocnik. He then assumed
command of Belzec and was later appointed inspector of the *Aktion Reinhard*
death camps. During his appointment the complete extermination system
was developed in the three camps and he oversaw the murder of millions.

Post Treblinka:
In September 1943 he was posted to Trieste in Italy where he commanded
the *SS-Einsatzkommando R*, which was composed of former *Aktion Reinhard*
members. On 26 May 1944, partisans killed Wirth near Trieste. His grave
(no 716) is marked by a large cross in the German Military Cemetery at
Costermano, near Verona.

Treblinka Chief Architect

THOMALLA, Richard *SS-Hauptsturmführer*
23/10/1903–12/05/1945
Richard Thomalla was the 'architect' of Belzec. On 1 November 1941 the construction of Belzec started. It ended in March 1942. At first Polish workers were used, later they were replaced by Jews from the surrounding ghettos. In late April or early May 1942, an SS team arrived in the Treblinka area, toured the region, and determined the site where a death camp would be erected. He remained at Treblinka for eight weeks to oversee the construction.

Post Treblinka:
Thomalla was executed by NKWD (Russian Secret Service) in Jicin, Czechoslovakia on 12 May 1945.

Treblinka Camp Commandants

EBERL, Dr Irmfried *SS-Obersturmführer*
08/09/1910–16/02/1948
In 1941 he was Director of the Brandenburg euthanasia centre and by 1942 of the Bernburg euthanasia centre, where he made his career in the euthanasia programme. Just prior to his appointment to Treblinka he was at Sobibor, training for his commandant's post. In July 1942 he became the first Commandant of Treblinka, until September 1942.

Post Treblinka:
In 1944 he served in the *Wehrmacht*, and after the war in 1945 he moved to Blaubeuren. However, he was arrested, tried for war crimes and imprisoned in 1947 where he hanged himself in February 1948 during his pre-trial detention.

STANGL, Franz *SS-Hauptsturmführer* NSDAP-number: 6.370.447, SS-Number: 296.569
26/03/1908–28/06/1971

Stangl was at Sobibor extermination camp from March to September 1942. In September he became Commandant of Treblinka until August 1943. His service there was regarded as impeccable and he soon received an official commendation as the 'best commandant in Poland'.

Post Treblinka:
In late 1943 he was posted to northern Italy where he was assigned to concentration camp duties in San Sabba. He then served as commander of *Einsatz R II* in the areas of Fiume and Udine, where he was engaged in actions against partisans and local Jews. At the end of the war he concealed his identity. He was detained briefly by the US Army in 1945 and briefly imprisoned in Austria for his part in the euthanasia programme. He escaped to Italy and then spent three years living in Syria before going to Brazil in 1951. Tracked down by Simon Wiesenthal he was extradited to West Germany, tried and found guilty of mass murder in 1970 and sentenced to life imprisonment. He died of heart failure in Düsseldorf prison.

FRANZ, Kurt Hubert *SS-Untersturmführer* SS-Number: 319 906
17/01/1914–04/07/1998
On 27 August 1943 he became the third Commandant of Treblinka until November 1943. In spring 1942 (as *SS-Scharführer*) to Belzec. In August/September 1942 he was ordered to Treblinka where he took over the Ukrainian guard squads and eventually became Deputy Camp Commandant. On 21 June 1943 he was promoted *SS-Untersturmführer*.

Post Treblinka:
After the war he returned to his former occupation as a cook and worked in Düsseldorf for 14 years. He was arrested in 1959 and sentenced to life in 1965. He was released in 1993 because of failing health and died in 1998.

SS Camp Personnel

ARNDT, Kurt (perhaps Paul) *SS-Unterscharführer*
Dates of birth and death unknown

Main duties in Camp II. Records are limited but his time at Treblinka was relatively short because he spoke about the activities there in a bar and was sent to the Sachsenhausen concentration camp.

Post Treblinka:
Details are unknown, but it is more than likely he died in the concentration camp.

BÄER, Rudolf *SS-Unterscharführer*
28/03/1906–unknown
Originally a carpenter. He moved through the ranks of the Waffen-SS he was eventually posted to Treblinka where he became the camp's bookkeeper and accountant in the camp office, located in Stangl's barrack.

Post Treblinka:
He served at Belzec as the camp's auditor. In May 1945 he fell into enemy hands and was detained at a POW camp Kirchbach in Kärnten, Austria before going into hiding. Further details about him are not presently known.

BIALA, Max *SS-Rottenführer*
05/08/1905–11/09/1942
He was deputy to Eberl from 23 July 1942–11 September 1942. He was stabbed on 11 September 1942, by a prisoner. After his murder the Ukrainian guards had their barracks in Treblinka named after him, calling it 'Max Biala *Kaserne*'.

BOELITZ, Lothar *SS-Unterscharführer*
Dates unknown
His main duties were in Camp II. He also was part of the squad that received prisoners on the platform when deportations arrived.

BOOTZ, Helmut
25/06/1907–unknown
Supervisor of the camp guards in Treblinka.

BOROWSKI, Werner *SS-Untersturmführer*
23/10/1913–unknown
After leaving Belzec he was appointed to Treblinka to become head of the economics section. He was later removed back to Bernburg because of the typhus epidemic.

Post Treblinka:
He was killed in action.

BREDOW, Paul *SS-Unterscharführer*
1902–1945
He belonged to a police detachment and was apparently from Silesia (*Schlesien*). Profession: male nurse. Served at Grafeneck and Hartheim. He arrived at the camp with Stangl and served there until spring 1943. He was Head of 'Barracks A', the clothing sorting barracks.

Post Treblinka:
In late 1943 was posted to San Sabba, Trieste in Italy. After the war in December 1945 he was killed in an accident in Göttingen.

EISELT, Karl
No service records are available at present.

EISOLD, Johannes
13/11/1907–unknown
At the camp he was put in charge of the excavators in order to move and bury the corpses.

Post Treblinka:
After Treblinka he served in Trieste in Italy. Records of him are limited.

EMMERICH, Rudolf
Dates unknown
No service records are available at present, but what is known through diaries is that he oversaw the operations and movements of the trains from Treblinka village station into the death camp.

FELFE, Hermann

04/01/1902–15/10/1947

Oversaw the construction of the first water tower in Camp I. According to records his time at the camp was short.

Post Treblinka:

The NKWD arrested him in 1945 and sentenced him to death in the Dresdner Ärzteprozess.

FLORIAN, (first name unknown)

Dates unknown

Appointed as a guard at the camp and served there for a short period.

FLOSS, Herbert SS-Scharführer

25/08/1912–22/10/1943

Had been appointed to all the Reinhard camps and was commander of Camp II in Treblinka. He was regarded as a cremation expert and was in charge of the arrangements for cremating the corpses. It is estimated that he cremated about 700,000 corpses.

Post Treblinka:

He was killed by Ukrainian guards in Zawadowka near Chelm in 1943.

FORKER, Alfred

31/07/1904–unknown

He was posted to Treblinka in 1942 and undertook guard duties in Camp II. His duties also encompassed the sorting yard as well.

Post Treblinka:

After Treblinka and Sobibor he was sent to Italy. Records are incomplete.

FUCHS, Erich *SS-Unterscharführer*

09/04/1902 (19/04/1902 (BDC))–25/07/1980 (1984 (BDC))

In 1941 he was drafted into the T-4 programme and worked as Dr Eberl's driver in the gassing centres Brandenburg and Bernburg. In July 1942 he was appointed to Treblinka where he was ordered by Wirth to install another gassing engine.

Post Treblinka:
In late 1942 he left the camp and worked for an oil company in Riga. In the last months of the war he became a member of the Waffen-SS in a tank transport unit. In May 1945 he was held in a Soviet POW camp, and then was employed by the British as a driver/mechanic in Bergen Belsen. In April 1963 he was arrested and finally three years later sentenced to four years imprisonment for being an accessory to the murder of at least 79,000 people. He died in Koblenz.

GENTZ, Ernst *SS-Unterscharführer*
Dates unknown
He was a guard who received prisoners on the platform when deportations arrived. In 1943 he was posted to Sobibor.

GROSSMANN, Willy *SS-Rottwachmeister*
26/01/1901–unknown
His guard training was undertaken at Pirna and the Trawniki training camp before finally being posted to Treblinka. His main duties were in Camp II and he also received prisoners on the platform when deportations arrived.

Post Treblinka:
In late 1943 he was sent back to Berlin and then was posted to Trieste where he fought against partisans. He also served in Telmezzo, Italy as guard of ammunition dump.

HACKENHOLT, Lorenz *SS-Hauptscharführer*
25/06/1914–31/12/1945
He assisted in the construction and operation of the gas chambers at Belzec. He also assisted in building gas chambers at Sobibor. Whilst he was at Belzec plans for the new gas chamber at Treblinka were drawn up by Hackenholt. He also assisted in laying the gas pipes for the Treblinka gas chambers.

Post Treblinka:
Served in Italy and survived the war. Was never brought to justice for his criminal acts.

HENGST, August *SS-Unterscharführer*
25/04/1905–unknown
He was an SS cook at Treblinka in the spring of 1942. He then served as a
relief cook.

Post Treblinka:
He was posted with fighting units to Italy. Because of bad health he was
then sent to Trieste as cook and then to San Sabba. He served there until
Italy surrendered on 10 May 1945.

HILLER, Richard *SS-Unterscharführer*
Dates unknown
He worked in the administration at both Sobibor and Treblinka. At
Treblinka he was posted to Camp I.

HIRTREITER, Josef *SS-Scharführer*
01/02/1909–27/11/1978
He was appointed to Treblinka in October 1942 until October 1943. His
main duties were in Camp II.

Post Treblinka:
In October 1943 he was ordered to Italy where he had to join an anti-
partisan police unit. After the war he was arrested in July 1946, and accused
of having served at the euthanasia centre Hadamar. On 3 March 1951 he
was sentenced to life imprisonment. He was the first man brought to trial
for crimes committed at Treblinka. Among the crimes he was found guilty
of was murdering young children aged between one and two, during the
unloading of the transports, by seizing them by the feet and smashing their
heads against the boxcars.

HÖDL, Franz *SS-Scharführer* SS-Number: 302 133
01/08/1905–unknown
Service records of his appointment at Treblinka are not presently known,
but what is known through diaries is that he probably operated the gassing
motors.

Post Treblinka:
He was ordered to Italy.

HORN, Otto *Richard* *SS-Unterscharführer*
14/12/1903–unknown
Following two weeks training at Trawniki in October 1942 he was sent
to Treblinka and supervised what became known as the *Grubenkommando*
(piling up the corpses, covering them with sand and Choleric lime) in the
extermination area, at the mass graves and at the incinerator where the
corpses of the victims were cremated later.

Post Treblinka:
He left Treblinka after the uprising in September 1943, and a few months
later was sent to Italy. After the war he attended the Treblinka trials in 1965,
one of ten brought to trial, but was acquitted.

KAINA, Erwin
24/03/1910–31/10/1942
In July/August 1942 he was ordered to form a work-brigade and supervise
the killings in Camp II.

Post Treblinka:
He committed suicide, dying in hospital at Ostrow Mazowiecki in October
1942.

KLAHN, Johannes *SS-Unterscharführer*
26/09/1908–unknown
He was assigned to Camp I for guard duties.

KLINZMANN, Willi
Dates unknown
There are no official records of him at present but it is known he was
appointed briefly to Treblinka, probably as a guard.

KÜTTNER, Fritz *SS-Oberscharführer* (also nicknamed 'Kiva' or 'Kiwe')
1907–unknown
He was Commander of Camp I.

Post Treblinka:
Posted to Italy. After the war he was arrested for war crimes but died before his trial started.

LAMBERT, Erwin Hermann *SS-Unterscharführer*
07/12/1909–unknown
Assigned to oversee the building of the barracks in July/August 1942. He also supervised a group of labourers and oversaw the construction of the gas chambers that were built in August 1942.

Post Treblinka:
In late 1943 he was posted to Italy and in March 1962 was arrested. He stood at what became known as the first Treblinka trial in 1965, and was sentenced to four years in prison.

LINDENMÜLLER, Alfons *SS-Hauptscharführer*
20/01/?–27/07/1946
He served at Treblinka in 1942 and was in charge of the *Goldjuden*. He left before the end of the year.

Post Treblinka:
He was arrested at the end of the war and died in a POW camp at Ksawera Koszelew in Poland.

LÖFFLER, Alfred *SS-Unterscharführer*
15/09/1904–30/04/1944
He served as a guard at Camp II.

Post Treblinka:
Details are limited, but what is known that he died during operations in Italy and is buried in the German Military Cemetery at Costermano, near Verona in Italy.

LUDWIG, Karl Emil *SS-Scharführer*
23/05/1906–1963
He was assigned guard duties in Camp II. In early 1943 records show that he was in charge of the *Waldkommando* at times in Camp III.

Post Treblinka:
In late 1943 he was posted to Italy. After the war he was acquitted at his trial, owing to the testimonies of Jewish witnesses.

MATTHES, Heinrich Arthur *SS-Scharführer*
11/01/1902–unknown
He was posted to the camp in August 1942 where he was appointed chief officer commanding Camp II and the gas chambers. He remained at Treblinka for over a year.

Post Treblinka:
After serving at Treblinka he was posted to Sobibor until late 1943. In early 1944 he was transferred to Italy as a policeman combating partisan activities and serving as a guard until the end of the war. After the war he led a relatively quiet existence until he was arrested for war crimes and was tried at the first Treblinka trial in 1965. He was found guilty and sentenced to life imprisonment.

MÄTZIG, Willy *SS-Oberscharführer*
06/08/1910–1993
He was book-keeper/accountant and was one of Stangl's two senior administrative assistants. His office was in Stangl's quarters. He was also part of the squad that received prisoners on the platform when deportations arrived.

Post Treblinka:
At the end of 1943 he was posted to Italy until the end of the war. There are no further records of him found at present.

MEIDKUR, Kurt *SS-Unterscharführer*
Dates unknown
Records are limited but he served at the camp, probably receiving prisoners on the platform when deportations arrived.

MENTZ, Willi *SS-Unterscharführer*
30/04/1904–unknown
He was assigned to Camp II in the summer of 1942 and then to Camp I as chief *Landwirtschaftskommando* (Agricultural Command).

Post Treblinka:
In December 1943 he was sent to work at Sobibor and then in early 1944 was posted to Italy to take part in what was known as the final action of *Aktion R* (persecution of Jews and partisans). After the war at the first Treblinka trial he was sentenced to life imprisonment.

MICHEL, Hermann *SS-Oberscharführer*
10/11/1901–unknown
He oversaw and received prisoners on the platform when deportations arrived and welcomed his victims with a short speech.

Post Treblinka:
Was captured by the US Army at Bad Aiblingen in Bavaria, but released on 19 April 1946.

MIETE, August Wilhelm *SS-Unterscharführer*
01/11/1908–unknown
He served at the camp between June 1942 and November 1943. He was assigned to Camp I at the 'Station', at the 'Undressing Yard'.

Post Treblinka:
At the end of 1943 he was posted to Italy where he was attached to a demolition unit. He was arrested in 1960 and was imprisoned on remand in Germany for five years until the first Treblinka trial. He was sentenced to life imprisonment and died in prison.

MÖLLER, Max *SS-Unterscharführer*
Dates unknown
Posted to Camp I as ordinance, 'Undressing Yard', and farming.

Post Treblinka:
Records of him are limited but he was posted to Italy in late 1943.

MÜNZBERGER, Gustav *SS-Unterscharführer* SS-Number: 321 758
17/08/1903–23/03/1977
From September 1942 until late 1943 he assisted in the operation of the gas chambers. He was in charge of *Leichentransportkommando* (Body-Transport Team).

Post Treblinka:
He was sent to Italy at the end of 1943. After the war he was arrested in July 1963. He was tried at the first Treblinka trial and was sentenced to twelve years in prison. He was released in 1971.

PLIKAT, Karl-Heinz
14/05/1907–01/05/1945
In 1942 was assigned to Camp I

Post Treblinka:
Records are limited. He was posted to Italy at the end of 1943.

POST, Philipp *SS-Unterscharführer*
Dates unknown
Posted to Camp I as weapons guard.

Post Treblinka:
Served in Italy and died in 1964.

PÖTZINGER, Karl *SS-Scharführer*
1908–22/12/1944
He was posted to the camp in 1942 and was in charge of the cremations in Camp II.

Post Treblinka:
After his posting to Italy in late 1943 he was killed in an air-raid the following year.

RICHTER, Kurt *SS-Scharführer*
1914–13/08/1944
In early 1943 he was posted to the camp as cook.

Post Treblinka:
At the end of 1943 he was sent to Italy and killed months later by partisans.

'ROSHA', *SS-Unterscharführer*
Dates unknown
Assigned to guard duties in Camp II.

ROST, Paul *SS-Untersturmführer* SS-Number: 382 366
12/06/1904–21/03/1984
In late 1942 he was sent from Sobibor to Treblinka and was put in charge of Camp II.

Post Treblinka:
At the end of 1943 he was posted to Italy. After the war he was imprisoned by the Soviets until the summer of 1946. He was then released and lived in Dresden until his death.

RUM, Franz Albert *SS-Unterscharführer*
08/06/1890–1970
Posted to the camp in late 1942. He became a guard for the *Leichentransportkommando* (Body-Transport Team) in Camp II. He was also head of 'Sorting Barracks B' in the Sorting Yard.

Post Treblinka:
In late 1943 he was sent to Italy. After the war at the first Treblinka trial he was sentenced to three years in prison. He died before beginning his sentence.

SCHARFE, Herbert ('Mischke') *SS-Unterscharführer*
13/02/1913–unknown
In 1942 he was put in charge of the camouflage command.

Post Treblinka:
There are limited records available, but it is more than likely he was posted to Italy in late 1943.

SCHEMMEL, Ernst *Polizeihauptmann* and *SS-Scharführer*
11/09/1883–10/12/1943
In 1942 he was posted to the camp where he served in the administration section for a short period.

Post Treblinka:
Records of him are limited, but what is known is that he died in Dresden at the end of 1943.

SCHIFFNER, Karl *SS-Unterscharführer* SS-Number: 321 225
04/07/1901–unknown
He was posted to the camp in 1942 and was in charge of the camp joinery and building team.

Post Treblinka:
After spending a short time at Treblinka he was sent to Belzec and then to Italy at the end of 1943 where he served in a police unit combating partisan activities until the end of the war. He was captured by the British and made a POW. He was released in late 1945.

SCHMIDT, Fritz *SS-Unterscharführer*
29/11/1906–04/02/1982
In 1942 he was pute in charge of the garage and operated the gas chamber engines. He was also commander of the camp metal works.

Post Treblinka:
In late 1943 he was posted to Italy. After the war in 1949 he was sentenced to nine years in prison. However, he never served his sentence because he escaped and went to West Germany, where he later died.

SCHUH, Richard *SS-Unterscharführer*, SS-Number. 98020
Dates unknown
In the summer of 1942 arrived at the camp and served in Camp 1. No other details are known.

SCHULZ, Erich
Dates unknown
From Sobibor he was posted to Treblinka as a guard.

Post Treblinka:
In late 1943 was sent to Italy. No other details are known.

SEIDEL, Kurt *SS-Obersturmführer*
20/03/1910–1972
He was in charge of road building. The main road in the camp was named after him, 'Kurt Seidel Straße'. He was also assigned to Camp II.

STADIE, Otto *SS-Stabsscharführer*
10/03/1897–unknown
He was posted to the camp in July 1942 and until July 1943 was in charge of the camp's administration. He was also part of the SS squad that received the prisoners into the camp.

Post Treblinka:
In August/September 1943 he was posted to Italy. After the war he was arrested and appeared in the dock at the first Treblinka trial in 1965. He was sentenced to six years in prison. He was later released from prison because of illness.

STENGELIN, Erwin *SS-Unterscharführer*
10/08/1911–14/10/1943
In the summer of 1942 he was posted to Treblinka and assigned to duties in camp.

Post Treblinka:
In 1943 he was sent to Sobibor and was killed in the uprising.

STREBELOW, Rudolf *SS-Zugführer*
Dates unknown
In the summer of 1942 he was posted to Treblinka and assigned to duties in Camp I.

SUCHOMEL, Franz *SS-Unterscharführer*
03/12/1907–unknown
Sent to the camp in August 1942 where he remained until late October 1943. His duties included the 'Station', then as supervisor in the female undressing barrack leading the victims to the 'tube'. In 1943 he was put in charge of the *Goldjuden* and the tailor shop.

Post Treblinka:
In late October 1943 he was posted to Sobibor and then after the uprising to Italy. He was later captured by US troops and in August 1945 released from the POW camp. He attended the first Treblinka trial and was sentenced to seven years in prison. He was released in 1969.

SYDOW, Franz (or perhaps Hermann) *SS-Unterscharführer*
1908–unknown
Sent to the camp in the summer of 1942 and was in charge of the camouflage commando.

Post Treblinka:
In late 1943 he was posted to Italy.

ZÄNKER, Hans
Dates unknown
Served at Treblinka as a guard. No other details are available at present.

Information obtained from ARC www.deathcamps.org

Appendix II

SS Personnel who served in 'Aktion Reinhard' Death Camps

Name	SS Rank	T4 Service	Aktion Reinhard Camp
Arndt, Kurt	SS–Scharführer	Hadamar	Treblinka
Bär, Rudolf	SS–Scharführer	Bernburg	Belzec, Treblinka
Barbl, Heinrich	SS–Scharführer	Hartheim	Belzec, Sobibor
Bauch, Ernst	SS–Unterscharführer	Bernburg, Sonnenstein	Sobibor
Bauer, Hermann Erich	SS–Oberscharführer		Sobibor
Baumann, Max	SS–Scharführer		Not in Belzec
Becher, Werner	SS–Unterscharführer	Sonnenstein	Sobibor
Beckmann, Rudolf	SS–Oberscharführer	Hartheim?	Sobibor
Beulich, Max	SS–Scharführer	Sonnenstein	Sobibor
Biela, Max	SS–Scharführer	Bernburg, Brandenburg	Treblinka
Boelitz,	SS–Unterscharführer		Treblinka
Blaurock, Kurt	SS–Scharführer	Sonnenstein	Sobibor
Bolender, Kurt	SS–Oberscharführer	Brandenburg, Hadamar, Hartheim, Sonnenstein	Sobibor, Lublin airfield
Bootz, Helmut	SS–Scharführer	Bernburg, Grafeneck	Treblinka? Sobibor?
Börner, Gerhardt	SS–Untersturmführer	Sonnenstein	Sobibor?
Borowski, Werner	SS–Untersturmführer	Bernburg	Treblinka, Belzec
Bredow, Paul;	SS–Unterscharführer	Grafeneck, Hartheim	Sobibor, Treblinka
Bree, Max	SS–Scharführer	Grafeneck, Hadamar	Sobibor, Treblinka

Name	SS Rank	T4 Service	Aktion Reinhard Camp
Dachsel, Arthur	Oberwachtmeister	Sonnenstein	Belzec, Sobibor
Dietze, Erich	SS-Scharführer	Ditto	Sobibor
Dubois, Werner	SS-Oberscharführer	Bernburg, Hadamar	Belzec, Sobibor
Eberl, Irmfried (Dr)	SS-Obersturmführer	Bernburg, Brandenburg	Sobibor, Treblinka
Eisold, Johannes	SS-Scharführer	Sonnenstein	Treblinka
Feix, Reinhold	SS-Untersturmführer		Belzec
Felfe, Hermann	SS-Scharführer	Grafeneck, Sonnenstein	Treblinka
Fichtner, Erwin	SS-Scharführer	Bernburg	Belzec
Floss, Herbert	SS-Scharführer	Bernburg	Belzec, Sobibor, Treblinka
Forker, Albert	SS-Scharführer	Sonnenstein	Treblinka, Sobibor
Franz, Kurt	SS-Untersturmführer	Brandenburg, Grafeneck, Sonnenstein	Belzec, Treblinka, Sobibor
Frenzel, Karl	SS-Untersturmführer	Bernburg, Grafeneck, Hadamar	Sobibor
Fuchs, Erich	SS-Unterscharführer	Bernburg, Brandenburg	Belzec, Sobibor, Treblinka
Gentz, Ernst	SS-Scharführer		Treblinka, Sobibor
Getzinger, Anton	SS-Oberscharführer	Hartheim	Sobibor
Girtzig, Hans	SS-Scharführer	Grafeneck, Hartheim	Belzec, Sobibor
Gley, Heinrich	SS-Oberscharführer	Grafeneck, Sonnenstein	Belzec
Gomerski, Herbert	SS-Unterscharführer	Hadamar	Sobibor
Graetschus, Siegfried	SS-Oberscharführer	Bernburg	Treblinka, Sobibor
Gringers, Max	SS-Scharführer	Hartheim	Belzec
Grömer, Ferdinand	SS-Scharführer	Hartheim	Sobibor
Grossmann, Willi	SS-Scharführer	Hadamar, Sonnenstein	Treblinka
Groth, Paul	SS-Unterscharführer	Hartheim	Belzec, Sobibor
Hackel, Emil	SS-Scharführer	Sonnenstein	Sobibor
Hackenholt, Lorenz	SS-Hauptscharführer	Grafeneck Sonnenstein	Belzec, Sobibor, Treblinka
Hengst, August	SS-Scharführer	Bernburg, Brandenburg	Treblinka
Hering, Gottlieb	Kriminalkommissar, SS-Hauptsturmführer	Bernburg, Hadamar, Hartheim, Sonnenstein	Belzec
Hiller, Richard	SS-Unterscharführer		Treblinka, Sobibor

Name	SS Rank	T4 Service	Aktion Reinhard Camp
Hirche, Fritz	Kriminal-Inspektor, SS-Unterscharführer	Hartheim	Belzec
Hirtreiter, Josef	SS-Unterscharführer	Hadamar	Treblinka, Sobibor
Hödl, Franz	SS-Unterscharführer	Hartheim	Sobibor
Horn, Otto	SS-Unterscharführer	Sonnenstein	Treblinka, Sobibor
Jirmann, Fritz	SS-Oberscharführer		Belzec
Ittner, Jakob	SS-Oberscharführer	T4-HQ Berlin	Sobibor
Jührs, Robert	SS-Unterscharführer	Hadamar	Belzec, Sobibor
Kainer, Erwin	SS-Scharführer	Hadamar	Treblinka
Kamm, Rudolf	SS-Scharführer	Sonnenstein	Belzec, Sobibor
Chelminski, Otto	SS-Scharführer		Belzec
Klahn, Johannes	SS-Scharführer	Sonnenstein	Treblinka, Sobibor
Klier, Johann	SS-Unterscharführer	Hadamar	Sobibor
Kloß, Walter	SS-Scharführer	Sonnenstein	Belzec
Konrad, Fritz	SS-Scharführer	Grafeneck, Sonnenstein	Sobibor
Kraschewski, Fritz	SS-Scharführer	Grafeneck, Hadamar?	Belzec
Küttner, Kurt	SS-Oberscharführer		Treblinka
Lachmann, Erich	SS-Scharführer		Sobibor
Lambert, Erwin	SS-Unterscharführer	Bernburg, Hadamar, Hartheim, Sonnenstein	Sobibor, Treblinka
Lindenmüller, Alfons	SS-Hauptscharführer		Treblinka
Löffler, Alfred	SS-Unterscharführer		Treblinka, Majdanek
Ludwig, Karl	SS-Scharführer	T4-HQ Berlin	Sobibor, Treblinka
Matthes, Heinrich	SS-Scharführer	Sonnenstein	Treblinka, Sobibor
Mätzig, Willi	SS-Oberscharführer	Bernburg, Brandenburg	Treblinka, Sobibor
Mentz, Willi	SS-Unterscharführer	Grafeneck, Hadamar	Treblinka, Sobibor
Meidkur, Kurt	SS-Unterscharführer		Treblinka
Michel, Hermann	SS-Oberscharführer	Grafeneck, Hartheim	Sobibor
Miete, August	SS-Scharführer	Grafeneck, Hadamar	Treblinka
Möller, Max	SS-Unterscharführer		Treblinka
Müller, Adolf	SS-Unterscharführer		Sobibor
Münzberger, Gustav	SS-Unterscharführer	Sonnenstein	Treblinka
Niemann, Johann	SS-Untersturmführer	Bernburg	Belzec, Sobibor
Nowak, Walter	SS-Scharführer	Sonnenstein	Sobibor

Name	SS Rank	T4 Service	Aktion Reinhard Camp
Oberhauser, Josef	SS-Oberscharführer	Bernburg, Brandenburg, Grafeneck, Sonnenstein	Belzec
Plikat, Karl- Heinz			Treblinka
Post, Phillipp	SS-Unterscharführer	Hadamar	Treblinka, Sobibor?
Pötzinger, Karl	SS-Unterscharführer	Bernburg, Brandenburg	Treblinka, Sobibor
Rehwald, Wenzel	SS-Unterscharführer	Bernburg, Hadamar, Harteim, Sonnenstein	Sobibor
Richter, Karl	SS-Scharführer	Hartheim, Sonnenstein	Sobibor, Treblinka
Reichleitner, Franz	SS-Haupsturmführer	Hartheim	Sobibor
Rost, Paul	SS-Unterscharführer	Hartheim, Sonnenstein	Sobibor, Treblinka
Rum, Franz	SS-Scharführer	T4-HQ Berlin	Treblinka, Sobibor?
Schäfer, Herbert	Brought Barry from Trawniki to Sobibor		Sobibor
Scharfe, Herbert	SS-Scharführer	Sonnenstein	Sobibor
Schemmel, Ernst	Kriminal-Obersekretär, SS-Scharführer	Hartheim, Sonnenstein	Sobibor, Treblinka
Schiffner, Karl	SS-Unterscharführer	Sonnenstein	Belzec, Sobibor, Treblinka
Schluch, Karl	SS-Unterscharführer	Grafeneck, Hadamar	Belzec
Schmidt, Fritz	SS-Scharführer	Bernburg, Sonnenstein	Treblinka
Schulz, Erich	SS-Scharführer	Grafeneck, Hadamar, Sonnenstein	Sobibor, Treblinka
Schütt, Hans-Heinz	SS-Scharführer	Grafeneck, Hadamar	Sobibor
Schwarz, Gottfried	SS-Untersturmführer	Bernburg, Grafeneck	Belzec
Seidel, Kurt	SS-Scharführer	Sonnenstein	Treblinka
Sporleder, Erich		Brandenburg	Belzec, Sobibor
Stadie, Otto	SS-Scharführer	Bernburg	Treblinka
Stangl, Franz	SS-Hauptsturmführer	Bernburg, Hartheim	Sobibor, Treblinka
Steffl, Thomas	SS-Scharführer	T4-HQ Berlin	Sobibor
Stengelin, Erwin	SS-Unterscharführer	Hadamar	Treblinka, Sobibor
Steubel, Karl	SS-Scharführer	Hartheim	Sobibor
Suchomel, Franz	SS-Scharführer	Hadamar	Treblinka, Sobibor
Sydow, Franz	SS-Unterscharführer		Treblinka, Sobibor

Name	SS Rank	T4 Service	Aktion Reinhard Camp
Tauscher, Friedrich	SS-Oberscharführer	Brandenburg, Hartheim, Sonnenstein	Belzec
Thomalla, Richard	SS-Haupsturmführer		Belzec, Sobibor, Treblinka
Unverhau, Heinrich	SS-Oberscharführer	Grafeneck, Hadamar	Belzec, Sobibor
Vallaster, Josef	SS-Scharführer	Hartheim	Belzec, Sobibor
Vey, Kurt	SS-Scharführer	Sonnenstein	Belzec, Sobibor
Wagner, Gustav	SS-Oberscharführer	Hartheim	Sobibor
Walther, Arthur	SS-Scharführer	Hartheim, Sonnenstein	Sobibor
Weiss, Otto	SS-Scharführer		Sobibor
Wendland, Wilhelm	SS-Scharführer	Sonnenstein	Sobibor
Wirth, Christian	SS-Sturmbannführer	Brandenburg, Grafeneck, Hadamar, Hartheim	Belzec
Wolf, Franz	SS-Unterscharführer	Hadamar	Sobibor
Wolf, Josef	SS-Unterscharführer		Sobibor
Zänker, Hans	SS-Scharführer	Sonnenstein	Belzec, Treblinka
Zaspel, Fritz	SS-Scharführer	Sonnenstein	Sobibor
Zierke, Ernst	SS-Unterscharführer	Grafeneck, Hadamar, Sonnenstein	Belzec, Sobibor

Reproduced courtesy of ARC www.deathcamps.org

Appendix III

Deportations to Treblinka from the General Government and Bialystok General District

Deportations from the General Government

County	Town	Date of deportation	Number of deportees
A. District of Warzaw			
Warzaw	Warzaw	22 July–28 August 1942	199,500
		3–12 September	52,000
		21 September	2,200
		18–22 January 1943	6,000
		19 April–15 May	7,000
	Falenica	19–20 August 1942	6,500
	Otwock	19–20 August 1942	7,000
	Rembertow	19–20 August 1942	1,800
	Ludwisin	19–20 August 1942	3,000
	Radzymin	19–20 August 1942	3,000
	Wolomin	19–20 August 1942	2,200
	Jadow	19–20 August 1942	700
Garwolin	Laskarzew	27 September	1,240
	Parysow	2 October	3,440
	Sobienie-Jeziory	2 October	3,680

County	Town	Date of deportation	Number of deportees
	Sobolew	2 October	1,640
	Zelechow	2 October	10,000
Minsk-Mazowiecki	Minsk-Mazowiecki	21–22 August	6,120
	Kaluszyn	15–27 September	6,000
	Kolbiel	15–27 September	1,000
	Mrozy Kuflew	15–27 September	1,000
	Siennica	15–27 September	700
	Stanislawow	15–27 September	700
Siedlce	Siedlce	22–24 August	11,700
		26 September	
		30 November	
	Losice	22 August	5,500
	Mordy	22 August	3,800
Sokolow-Wegrow	Sokolow-Podlaski	22–25 September	5,800
	Wegrow	22–25 September	8,300
	Kosow-Lacki	22–25 September	1,100
	Sterdyn	22–25 September	1,100
	Stoczek	22–25 September	2,000
B. District of Radom			
Radom	Radom	5–17 August 1942	30,000
		13 January 1943	1,500
	Kozienice	27 September 1942	13,000
	(including Jews		
	from Glowaczow,		
	Magnuszew,		
	Marianpol,		
	Mniszew, Ryczywol,		
	Sieciechow,		
	Stromiec, Trzebien)		

County	Town	Date of deportation	Number of deportees
	Zwolen (including Jews from Garbatka, Janowice, Oblassy, Pionki, Policzna, Sarnow, Gniewoszow)	29 September	10,000
	Szydlowiec	24 September	10,000
		13 January 1943	5,000
	Gniewoszow (in addition to those sent through Zwolen)	15 November 1942	1,000
Kielce	Kielce	20–24 August	21,000
	Chechny	(?) September	4,000
	Skarzysko-Kamienna	21–22 September October (beginning)	2,500
	Suchedniow (including Jews from Bodzentyn)	21–22 September	4,000
Czestochowa	Czestochowa	21 September–5 October	40,000
Radomsko	Radomsko	10–12 October	14,000
		6 January	4,000
	Koniecpol	7 October 1942	1,600
	Zarki	6 October	800
Piotrkow	Piotrkow	15–25 October	22,000
	Gorzkowice	15–25 October	1,500
	Kamiensk	15–25 October	500
	Przyglow	15–25 October	2,000

County	Town	Date of deportation	Number of deportees
	Sulejow	15–25 October	1,500
Jerdrzejow	Jerdrzejow	16–25 September	6,000
	Sedziszow	16–25 September	1,000
	Szczekociny	16–25 September	1,500
	Wloszczowa	16–25 September	5,000
	Wodzislaw	16–25 September	3,000
Busko	Busko-Zdroj	1–5 October	2,000
	Chmielnik	1–5 October	8,000
	Nowy Korczyn	1–5 October	4,000
	Pacanow	1–5 October	3,000
	Pinczow	1–5 October	3,000
	Stopnica	5–6 November	5,000
Konskie	Konskie	3–7 November	9,000
	Gowarczow	3–7 November	1,000
	Przedborz	9–12 October	4,000
	Radoszyce	3 November	4,000
Tomaszow-Mazowiecki	Tomaszow-Mazowiecki	15 October–2 November	15,000
	Biala-Rawska	15 October–2 November	4,000
	Orzewicz	15 October–2 November	2,000
	Koluszki	15 October–2 November	3,000
	Nowe Miastro	15 October–2 November	3,000
	Opovzno	15 October–2 November	3,000
	Prysucha	15 October–2 November	4,000
	Rawa Mazowiecka	31 October	4,000
	Zarnow	31 October	2,000
	Ujazd	31 October	800
		6 January 1943	2,000
Starachowize	Starachowize	15–29 October 1942	4,500
	Chotcha Nowa	15–29 October	4,000
	Ciepielow	15–29 October	600
	Ilza	15–29 October	2,000

County	Town	Date of deportation	Number of deportees
	Lipsko	15–29 October	3,000
	Sienno	15–29 October	2,000
	Tarlow	15–29 October	7,000
	Wierzbnik	15–29 October	4,000
Opatow	Opatow	20 October	Numbers unknown
	Cmielow	October (end)	
	Iwaniska	15 October	
	Kunow	October (end)	
	Klimontow	30 October	
	Koprzywnica	31 October	
	Lagow	7 October	
	Osiek	25 October	
	Ostrowiec	11–12 October	
	Ozarow	October (end)	
	Staszow	7 November	
	Sandomierz	10 January 1943	

C. District of Lublin

County	Town	Date of deportation	Number of deportees
Biala-Podlaska	Biala-Podlaska	26 September–6 October 1942	4,800
Radzyn	Radzyn	1 October	2,000
	Lukow (including Jews from Adamow)	5–8 October	7,000
		7 November	3,000
	Miedzyrzec-Podalski	25–26 August	11,000
	Parczew (including Jews from Kock)	19–25 August	5,500

Deportations from Bialystok General District

Ghetto / Collection Camp (C.C.)	Details of Deportation from Ghettos or through Collection Camps	Date of deportation	Number of deportees
Bialystok ghetto	Five transports with 2,000 Jews each	9–13 February 1943	10,000
	The liquidation of the ghetto	18–19 August 1943	7,600
Bialystok C.C.	Knyszyn – 1,300 Grodek-Bialystocki – 1,380 Lapy – 450 Choroszcz – 440 Michalowo – 750 Sokoly – 850 Suprasl – 170 Wasilkow – 1,180 Zabludow – 1,400 Kleszczele – 400 Milejczyce – 1,000	10 November– 15 December 1942	9,320
Jasionowka	In the ghetto there were 400 Jews from surrounding localities	25 January 1943	2,120
Grodno	Over 10,000 Jews were deported in this action, most of them to Auschwitz, and one transport to Treblinka	18–22 January 1943	1,600
	The liquidation of the ghetto	14–19 February	4,400

Borgusze C.C.	Goniadz – 1,300 Trzcianne – 1,200 Augustow – 2,000 Grajewo – 2,500 Rajgrod – 500 Szcuczyn – 1,500	10 November– 15 December 1942	9,100
Kelbasin C.C.	Druskieniki – 500 Jeziory – 2,000 Lunna – 1,500 Ostryna – 2,000 Porzecze – 1,000 Skidel – 3,000 Sopockinie – 2,000 Dabrowa – 1,000 Indura – 2,500 Janow – 950 Krynki – 5,000 Kuznica – 1,000 Korycin – 1,000 Odelsk – 500 Sidra – 350 Sokolka – 8,000 Suchowola – 5,100 Grodno – 1,500	10 November– 15 December	38,900
Volkovysk C.C.	Jalowka – 850 Lyskow – 600 Mosty – 350 Porozow – 1,000 Ros – 1,000 Rozana – 3,000 Swislocz – 3,000 Wolkovysk – 7,000 Wolfa – 1,500 From this camp 2,000 were sent to Auschwitz and the rest to Treblinka	10 November– 15 December	16,300

County of Bielsk-Podlaski	In the ghetto of Bielsk-Podlaski there were 7,000 local Jews, and 4,000 more were brought there from Bocki, Bransk, Narew, and Orla. They were deported in eleven transports, 1,000 in each transport.	2–11 November	11,000
	Ghetto of Ciechanowiec	15 October	3,300
	Siemiatycze	2–10 November	4,330

Reproduced with kind permission from Yitzhak Arad's book *Belzec, Sobibor, Treblinka – The Operation Reinhard Death Camps*. Indiana University Press 1987

Appendix IV

List of Camps

Overleaf: Reproduced from About.com: 20th Century History

Hershl Sperling, one of the tiny number who survived Treblinka, with his son. For his whole extraordinary story, see *Treblinka Survivor* by Mark S. Smith.

Camp	Function	Location	Established	Evacuated	Liberated	Estimated number of victims
Auschwitz	Concentration/Extermination	Oswiecim, Poland (near Krakow)	26 May 1940	18 January 1945	27 January 1945 by Soviets	1,100,000
Belzec	Extermination	Belzec, Poland	March 17, 1942		Liquidated by Nazis December 1942	600,000
Bergen-Belsen	Detention; Concentration (After 3/44)	near Hanover, Germany	April 1943		15 April 1945 by British	35,000
Buchenwald	Concentration	Buchenwald, Germany (near Weimar)	16 July 1937	6 April 1945	11 April 1945 by Americans	56,000
Chelmno	Extermination	Chelmno, Poland	7 December 1941; 23 June 1944		Closed March 1943 (but reopened); liquidated by Nazis July 1944	320,000
Dachau	Concentration	Dachau, Germany (near Munich)	22 March 1933	26 April 1945	29 April 1945 by Americans	32,000
Dora/Mittelbau	Sub-camp of Buchenwald; Concentration (After 10/44)	near Nordhausen, Germany	27 August 1943	1 April 1945	9 April 1945 by Americans	Unknown
Drancy	Assembly/Detention	Drancy, France (suburb of Paris)	August 1941		17 August 1944 by Allied Forces	Unknown

Camp	Function	Location	Established	Evacuated	Liberated	Estimated number of victims
Flossenbürg	Concentration	Flossenbürg, Germany (near Nuremberg)	3 May 1938	20 April 1945	23 April 1945 by Americans	Unknown
Gross-Rosen	Sub-camp of Sachsenhausen; Concentration (After 5/41)	near Wroclaw, Poland	August 1940	13 February 1945	8 May 1945 by Soviets	40,000
Janowska	Concentration/ Extermination	L'viv, Ukraine	September 1941		Liquidated by Nazis November 1943	Unknown
Kaiserwald/Riga	Concentration (After 3/43)	Meza-Park, Latvia (near Riga)	1942	July 1944		Unknown
Koldichevo	Concentration	Baranovichi, Belarus	Summer 1942			22,000
Majdanek	Concentration/ Extermination	Lublin, Poland	16 February 1943	July 1944	22 July 1944 by Soviets	360,000
Mauthausen	Concentration	Mauthausen, Austria (near Linz)	8 August 1938		5 May 1945 by Americans	120,000
Natzweiler/ Struthof	Concentration	Natzweiler, France (near Strasbourg)	1 May 1941	September 1944		12,000

Camp	Function	Location	Established	Evacuated	Liberated	Estimated number of victims
Neuengamme	Sub-camp of Sachsenhausen; Concentration (After 6/40)	Hamburg, Germany	13 December 1938	29 April 1945	May 1945 by British	56,000
Plaszow	Concentration (After 1/44)	Krakow, Poland	October 1942	Summer 1944	15 January 1945 by Soviets	8,000
Ravensbrück	Concentration	near Berlin, Germany	15 May 1939	23 April 1945	30 April 1945 by Soviets	90,000, though some transferred to other camps
Sachsenhausen	Concentration	Berlin, Germany	July 1936	March 1945	27 April 1945 by Soviets	30,000
Sered	Concentration	Sered, Slovakia (near Bratislava)	1941/42		1 April 1945 by Soviets	Unknown
Sobibor	Extermination	Sobibor, Poland (near Lublin)	March 1942	Revolt on October 14, 1943; Liquidated by Nazis October 1943	Summer 1944 by Soviets	250,000

Camp	Function	Location	Established	Evacuated	Liberated	Estimated number of victims
Stutthof	Concentration (After 1/42)	near Danzig, Poland	2 September 1939	25 January 1945	9 May 1945 by Soviets	65,000
Theresienstadt	Concentration	Terezin, Czech Republic (near Prague)	24 November 1941	Handed over to Red Cross 3 May 1945	8 May 1945 by Soviets	33,000
Treblinka	Extermination	Treblinka, Poland (near Warsaw)	23 July 1942	Revolt on 2 April 1943; liquidated by the SS April 1943		800,000
Vaivara	Concentration/Transit	Estonia	September 1943		Closed 28 June 1944	Unknown
Westerbork	Transit	Westerbork, Netherlands	October 1939		12 April 1945 camp handed over to Kurt Schlesinger	Unknown

Appendix V

List of Ukrainian Guards

Trawniki concentration camp was an SS labour camp which sent labour to a nearby industrial plant. The Trawniki camp was commanded by SS-*Hauptsturmführer* Theodor von Eupen. It also trained Eastern European *Hiwi* (volunteers), for service with Nazi occupation forces in occupied Poland and neighbouring countries. Many of those that trained at Trawniki were posted to the Operation Reinhard camps. Below is a list of European Ukrainian Hiwis that were posted to Treblinka as guards and under the direct command of the SS.

Andreyev (supervised Yankiel Wiernik on the construction of the larger gas chambers in Treblinka, during the autumn of 1942)
Mikolaj Bondarenko
Peter Bondave
Dimitriy Borodin
Volodymr Cherniavshy
Piotr Dmitrenko
Fiodor Duszenko
Fedor Federenko
Pyoter Goncharov
Mikolaj Gonzural

Pavel Stepanovich Grigorchuk
Wasil Jelentschuk
Nikolai Kulak
Ivan Kurinnoy
Ananiy Grigoryevich Kuzminski
Nikolay Lebedenko
Pavel Vladimirovich Leleko
Filip Levchishin
Nikolay Makoda
Nikolay Petrovich Malagon
Ivan Ivanovych Marchenko
Moisei Martoszenko
Theodozy Melnik

Mikolaj Nidosrelow
Daniel Onoprijenko
Mikolaj Osyczanski
Aleksander Paraschenko
Yevdokim Parfinyuk
Nikolay Payevshchik
Pinneman
Leon Polakow
Samuil Martinovich Prits
(Prishch)
Alexander Rittich
Robertus
Boris Rogoza
Grigorij Rubez
Wasyl Rudenko
Fyodor Ryabeka
Prokofiy Ryabtsev
Mikolay Scheffer
Wasil Schischajew
Iwan Schmidkin
Aleksander Schultz (served in
Belzec and Treblinka)

Emanuel Genrikhov Schultz
(served at Treblinka and Sobibor)
Nikolay Senik
Mikolay Senykow
Nikolay Shalayev
Ivan Shevchenko
Ivan Danilovich Shvidkoy
Nikolay Skakodub
Grigoriy Skydan
Oswald Strebel
Ivan Terekhov
Ivan Tkachuk
Wladimir Tscherniewskij
Sergey Vasilenko
Aleksander Voleshenko
Iwan Wasilenko
Wasyl Woloszyn (served in Belzec
and Treblinka)
Vasily Woronkow
Alexander Ivanovich Yeger
Vasily Yelenchuk
Trofim Zavidenko

Appendix VI

Operation Reinhard Death Camps and the Estimated Death Toll

Belzec

The extermination camp commenced functioning in March 1942, and ceased operations in December 1942. A minimum of 435,000 Jews had been murdered there.

Sobibor

An extermination camp in eastern Poland near Lublin. It opened in May 1942, and while it functioned approximately 250,000 Jews were killed, until it finally closed after the prisoners revolted on 14 October 1943. Most of the escapees were subsequently captured and killed.

Treblinka

Situated in north-east Poland, between Warsaw and Bialystok. It commenced operations in July 1942. However, in the autumn of 1943 the SS destroyed the camp in order to conceal their crimes in the face of the advancing Red Army. Some 800,000 Jews had been killed.

Estimated total murdered: 1,485,000.

The following information as to how the death toll at Treblinka has been estimated is kindly provided by the remarkable anti-revisionist website, the Nizkor Project, www.nizkor.org.

The most accurate figures available regarding the numbers killed at the Treblinka camp are found in the judgements (*Urteilsbegrundung*) from the first and second Treblinka trials, held in Düsseldorf in 1965 and 1970. Passed on 3 September 1965 in the trial of Kurt Franz and nine others at the Court of Assizes in Düsseldorf (First Treblinka Trial) (iAZ-LG Dusseldorf. II 931638, p.49 ff), and the trial of Franz Stangl at the Court of Assizes at Düsseldorf (Second Treblinka Trial) on December 22, 1970 (AZ–LG Düsseldorf, XI-148/69 S, p.111 ff).

At least 700,000 persons, predominantly Jews, but also a number of Gypsies, were killed at the extermination camp. These findings are based on the expert opinion submitted to the Court of Assizes by Dr Helmut Krausnick, Director of the Institute for Contemporary History (*Institute für Zeitgeschichte*) in Munich. In formulating his opinion, Dr Krausnick consulted all the German and foreign archival material accessible to him and customarily studied in historical research. Among the documents he examined were the following:

1 The so-called Stroop report, a report by *SS-Brigadeführer* (Brigadier) Jurgen Stroop, dealing with the destruction of the Warsaw ghetto. This report consists of three parts: namely, an introduction, a compilation of daily reports and a collection of photographs.
2 The record of the trial of the major war criminals before the International Military Tribunal in Nuremberg.
3 The official transportation documents (train schedules, telegrams, and train inventories) relevant to the transports to Treblinka.

The latter documents, of which only a part were recovered after the war, were the subject of the trial and were made available to Dr Krausnick by the Court of Assizes. Dr Krausnick's report includes the following information: According to the Stroop report a total of approximately 310,000 Jews were transported in freight trains from the Warsaw ghetto to Treblinka during the period from 22 July 1942 to 3 October 1942.

Approximately another 19,000 Jews made the same journey during the period from January, 1943 to the middle of May, 1943. During the period from 21 August 1942 to 23 August 1943, additional transports of Jews arrived at the Treblinka extermination camp, likewise by freight train, from other Polish cities, including Kielce, Miedzyrec, Lukow, Wloszczowa, Sedzizzow, Czestochowa, Szydlowiec, Lochow, Kozienice, Bialystok, Tomaszow, Grodno and Radom. Other Jews, who lived in the vicinity of Treblinka, arrived at Treblinka in horse-drawn wagons and in trucks, as did Gypsies, including some from countries other than Poland. In addition, Jews from Germany and from other European countries, including Austria, Czechoslovakia, Bulgaria, Yugoslavia and Greece, were transported to Treblinka, predominantly in passenger trains.

It has not been possible, of course, to establish the exact number of people transported to Treblinka in this fashion, because only a part of the transportation documents, particularly those relevant to the railroad transports, are available. Still, assuming that each of the trains consisted of an average of 60 cars, with each freight car holding an average total of 100 persons and each passenger car an average total of 50 (i.e. that each freight train might have carried an approximate total of 6,000, and each passenger train an approximate total of 3,000 Jews to Treblinka) the total number of people transported to Treblinka in freight trains and passenger trains might be estimated at approximately 271,000. This total would not include the 329,000 from Warsaw. Actually, however, these figures in many instances were much larger than the ones cited above. Besides, many additional thousands of Jews – and also Gypsies – arrived in Treblinka in horse-drawn wagons and on trucks. Accordingly, it must be assumed that the total number of Jews from Warsaw, from other parts of Poland, from Germany and from other European countries who were taken to Treblinka, plus the total of at least 1,000 Gypsies who shared the same fate, amounted to far more than 700,000, even if one considers that several thousands of people were subsequently moved from Treblinka to other camps and that a number of inmates succeeded in escaping from the camp, especially during the revolt of 2 August 1943. In view of the foregoing, it would be scientifically admissible to estimate the total number of persons killed in Treblinka at a minimum of 700,000.

The Court of Assizes saw no reason to question the opinion of this expert, who was known in the scholarly world for his studies on the National

Socialist persecution of the Jews. The expert opinion he submitted was detailed, thorough and, therefore, convincing.

In the autumn of 1969 another expert, Dr Scheffler, submitted for the second Treblinka trial an opinion which was based on more recent research, estimating the total number of victims at about 900,000.

Appendix VII

Rank Equivalents

German Army	Waffen-SS	British Army
Gemeiner, Landser	Schütze	Private
	Oberschütze	
Grenadier	Sturmmann	Lance Corporal
Obergrenadier		
Gefreiter	Rottenführer	Corporal
Obergefreiter	Unterscharführer	
Stabsgefreiter		
Unteroffizier	Scharführer	Sergeant
Unterfeldwebel	Oberscharführer	Colour Sergeant
Feldwebel		
Oberfeldwebel	Hauptscharführer	Sergeant Major
Stabsfeldwebel	Hauptbereitschaftsleiter	
	Sturmscharführer	Warrant Officer
Leutnant	Untersturmführer	Second Lieutenant
Oberleutnant	Obersturmführer	First Lieutenant
Hauptmann	Hauptsturmführer	Captain

Major	Sturmbannführer	Major
Oberstleutnant	Obersturmbannführer	Lieutenant Colonel
Oberst	Standartenführer	Colonel
	Oberführer	Brigadier General
Generalmajor	Brigadeführer	Major General
Generalleutnant	Gruppenführer	Lieutenant General
General	Obergruppenführer	General
Generaloberst	Oberstgruppenführer	
Generalfeldmarschall	Reichsführer-SS	

Bibliography

Arad, Yitzhak, *Belzec, Sobibor, Treblinka: Operation Reinhard Death Camps,* Indiana University Press, 1987

Benz, Wolfgang, Graml, Hermann and Weiß, Hermann (eds), *Enzyklopädie des Nationalsozialismus,* Deutscher Taschenbuch Verlag, München, 2001

Blatt, Thomas, *Sobibor – The Forgotten Revolt,* H.E.P. Issaquah WA 1998

Böhm, Dr Boris et al. *Nationalsozialistische Euthanasieverbrechen in Sachsen* Kuratorium Gedenkstätte Sonnenstein e.V., 1996

Böhm, Dr Boris et al. *Sonnenstein Heft 3/2001,* Pirna: Kuratorium Gedenkstätte Sonnenstein e.V., 2001

Buchheim, Hans, Broszat, Martin, Jacobsen, Hans–Adolf, Krausnick, Helmut, *Anatomie des SS-Staates,* Deutscher Taschenbuch Verlag, Munich, 1967

Burba, Dr Manfred, *Treblinka: Ein NS-Vernichtungslager im Rahmen der 'Aktion Reinhard',* Göttingen, 2000

Chrostowski, Witold, *Extermination Camp Treblinka,* Valentine Mitchell, 2004

Dawidowicz, Lucy, *The War Against the Jews 1933–1945,* Holt, Rinehart and Winston, New York, 1975

Donat, Alexander (ed), *The Death Camp Treblinka* New York: Holocaust Library, 1979

Eberhard Jäckel, Peter Longerich, Julius H. Schoeps (eds), *Enzyklopädie des Holocaust. Die Verfolgung und Ermordung der europäischen Juden,* 3 vols., Argon Verlag, Berlin 1993

Fleming, Gerald, *Hitler and the Final Solution,* University of California Press, Berkeley, 1984

Friedlander, Saul, *Nazi Germany and the Jews: Volume 1 The Years of Persecution 1933–1939,* HarperPerennial, New York, 1997

Friedlander, Henry, *The Origins of Nazi Genocide: From Euthanasia to the Final Solution,* The University of North Carolina Press, 1995

Gilbert, Martin, *Atlas of the Holocaust,* William Morrow and Company, Inc., New York, 1993

Gilbert, Martin, *The Holocaust: the Jewish Tragedy,* Fontana/Collins, Glasgow, 1989

Glazar, Richard, *Trap with a Green Fence – Survival in Treblinka,* Northwestern University Press, 1999

Grossmann, Wassilij, *Die Hölle Von Treblinka,* Moscow: Verlag für fremdsprachige Literatur, 1947

Hilberg, Raul, *The Destruction of the European Jews,* Holmes & Meier, 1985

Hoffmann, *Dr Ute and Schulze,* Dietmar Gedenkstatte Bernburg

Kershaw, Ian, *Hitler 1936–1945: Nemesis,* Allen Lake The Penguin Press, London, 2000

Klee, Ernst (ed), *The Good Old Days: the Holocaust as seen by its perpetrators and bystanders,* The Free Press, 1991

Kogon, Eugen, *Der SS-Staat. Das System der deutschen Konzentrationslager,* Karl Alber Verlag, Munich, 1946

Krausnick, H., and Wilhelm, H.-H., *Die Truppe des Weltanschauungskrieges: Die Einsatzgruppen der Sicherheitspolizei und des SD, 1938-1942,* Stuttgart, 1981

Kuperhand, Miriam and Saul, *Shadows of Treblinka,* University of Illinois Press, 1998

Lanzman, Claude, *Shoah,* Da Capo Press, New York, 1995

Letter of the SS-Administrator of June 2, 1943 to the *Bauinspektion* (Construction Inspection Office) of the Waffen-SS and Police Reich-East, RGVA, 502-1-314

Marszałek, Józef '*Rozpoznanie obozów Śmierci w Bełzcu, Sobiborze, e Treblince przez wywiad Armii Krajowej i Delegatury Rządu Rzeczyspolitej Polskiej na Ktaju*' (The Reconnaissance of the Death Camps Bełżec, Sobibór, and Treblinka by the Intelligence Service of the Homeland Army and the Delegation of the Government of the Republic of Poland in the Country), in: *Biuletyn Głównej Komisji Badania Zbrodni przeciwko narodowi polskiemu / Instytutu Pamięci Narodowe,* Volume XXXV, Warsaw 1993

NSG-Prozeß 'Treblinka' in: *Historische Tatsachen* no. 12 ('*Das Recht, in dem wir leben*'), Vlotho 1982

Nuremberg Trial Proceedings Vol. 8 Sixty-Ninth Day, Wednesday, 27 February 1946

Poliakov, Léon, *Harvest of Hate*, Holocaust Library, New York 1979

Poprzeczny, Joseph, *Hitler's Man in the East – Odilo Globocnik*, McFarland & Co Inc Publishers, 2004

Reitlinger, Gerald, *The Final Solution: The Attempt to Exterminate the Jews of Europe 1939–1945*, Thomas Yoseloff, 1961

Rückerl, Adalbert, *NS-Vernichtungslager im Spiegel deutscher Strafprozesse*, DTV Dokumente, München, 1977

Schelvis, Jules, *Vernichtungslager Sobibor – UNRAST* Verlag Hamburg/Munster, 2003

Schilter, Thomas, *Unmenschliches Ermessen*, Leipzig Gustav Kiepenheuer Verlag, 1999

Sereny, Gitta, *Am Abgrund: Gespräche mit dem Henker – Franz Stangl und die Morde von Treblinka* München: R. Piper Verlag, 1995

Sereny, Gitta, *Into that Darkness – From Mercy Killing to Mass Murder,* London McGraw-Hill Book Company, 1974

Smith, Mark S., *Treblinka Survivor: The Life and Death of Hershl Sperling,* Spellmount, Stroud 2010

State of Israel. Ministry of Justice, *The Trial of Adolf Eichmann. Record of Proceedings in the District Court of Jerusalem* Jerusalem 1993

Steiner, Jean-Francois, *Treblinka,* Simon and Schuster, New York 1967

Teicholz, Tom, *The Trial of Ivan the Terrible: state of Israel vs. John Demjanjuk,* New York, St. Martin's Press, 1990

Tregenza, Michael, Christian Wirth: 'Inspekteur der Sonderkommandos, 'Aktion Reinhard" unpublished English article (published in Polish as: 'Zessyty Majdanka', Vol. XV, Lublin 1993)

Willenberg, Samuel, *Revolt in Treblinka,* Warsaw: Zydowski Instytut Historyczny, 1989

Willenberg, Samuel, *Surviving Treblinka,* Oxford: Basil Blackwell Ltd in association with the Institute for Polish-Jewish Studies, 1989

Witte, Peter and Tyas, Stephen, A New Document on the Deportation and Murder of Jews during 'Einsatz Reinhardt' 1942, in *Holocaust and Genocide Studies,* Volume 15, Issue 3: Winter 2001

Zentner, Christian and Bedürftig, Friedmann (eds), *The Encyclopedia of the Third Reich*, Da Capo Press, New York, 1997

Other Sources

Dr Boris Böhm, Sonnenstein Memorial
Dr Ursula Schwarz, DOEW
Dr Ute Hoffmann, Bernburg Memorial
Files of *Landgericht Hamburg* and *Landgericht Düsseldorf*
Berlin Document Centre, file 329/1
Schloss Kalkum archive, Düsseldorf
Dr Heinz-Ludger Borgert, Ludwigsburg archive
United States Holocaust Memorial Museum
About.com:20th Century History
ARC www.deathcamps.org
Holocaust Education and Archive Research Team (H.E.A.R.T.)
www.holocaustresearchproject.org

Endnotes

1 H.Krausnick and H.-H Wilhelm, *Die Truppe des Weltanschauungskrieges: Die Einsatzgruppen der Sicherheitspolizei und des SD, 1938 1942*, p.551

2. Sereny, Gitta, *Into that Darkness*, p.54

3. ibid, p.111

4. ibid, p.113–14

5. ibid, p.114

6. Document USS-344. GARF, 7445-2-126, p.320

7. Chrostowski, Witold, *Extermination Camp Treblinka* p.25–6

8. ibid, p.27

9. Diary extract from Grzegorz Wozniak Woz845/VOL.1/3685

10. Chrostowski, Witold, *Extermination Camp Treblinka,* p.31

11. Faschismus, op.cit. pp.305–7

12. Arad, Yitzhak, *Belzec, Sobibor, Treblinka. The Operation Reinhard Death Camps,* p.193

13. ibid, p.196

14. ibid, p.218

15. ibid, p.194

16. Glazar, p.47

17. Arad, Yitzhak, *Belzec, Sobibor, Treblinka. The Operation Reinhard Death Camps,* p.196

18. ibid, p.196

19. From the handwritten memoirs of Rudolf Höss – Reminiscenses/96,

volume 1–5, inventory number 49757 (Auschwitz-Birkenau Museum)

20. Arad, Yitzhak, *Belzec, Sobibor, Treblinka. The Operation Reinhard Death Camps*, p.91–2

21. Sereny, Gitta, *Into that Darkness,* p.157

22. Arad, Yitzhak, *Belzec, Sobibor, Treblinka. The Operation Reinhard Death Camps,* p.92

23. Strawczinski, p.11–12

24. Arad, Yitzhak, *Belzec, Sobibor, Treblinka. The Operation Reinhard Death Camps,* p.96

25. Belzec – Oberhauser, Band 9, p.1713

26. Arad, Yitzhak, *Belzec, Sobibor, Treblinka. The Operation Reinhard Death Camps,* p.121

27. Rozenberg, p.6

28. Arad, Yitzhak, *Belzec, Sobibor, Treblinka. The Operation Reinhard Death Camps,* p.122

29. Ernest Klee, Willi Dressen, and Volker Riess, *The Good Old Days*, p.245–7

30. Chrostowski, Witold, *Extermination Camp Treblinka,* p.71

31. Sereny, Gitta, *Into that Darkness,* p.200

32. ibid, p.209–10

33. ibid, p.223

34. ibid, p.221

35. ibid, p.222

36. ibid, p.223–4

37. Arad, Yitzhak, *Belzec, Sobibor, Treblinka. The Operation Reinhard Death Camps,* p.168

38. Wiernik, Rok, W. *Treblinka,* p.35

39. Treblinka-Fraz, Band 10, p.2057

40. YVA, 0-3/3816 P41-42 Testimony of Yechiel Reichman

41. ibid, p.450–1

42. Sereny, Gitta, *Into that Darkness,* p.234–6

43. Extract from Ernst Reuss to Author. November 2008. Diary Catalogued 43216/A/2 ER

44. Wiernik, Rok. W. *Treblinka,* p.19

45. Extract from Ernst Reuss to author. November 2008. Diary Catalogued 43217/B/3 ER

46. Extract from Ernst Reuss to author. November 2008. Diary Catalogued 43218/C/4 ER

47. Sereny, Gitta, *Into that Darkness,* p.238
48. ibid, p.239
49. ibid, p.239
50. ibid, p.247
51. ibid, p.248
52. ibid, p.249
53. Zabecki, *Wspomnienia Dawne I Nowe,* p.97–8
54. ibid, p.97–8
55. Sereny, Gitta, *Into that Darkness,* p.261
56. Poliakov, L. and J. Wulf, *Das Dritte Reich und die Juden,* op.cit, p.44–5
57. ibid, p.45

Index